UNITY LIBRARY 8 ARCHIVES
The Gospel paradox.
BT 375.2 .J313

0 0251

W9-DCC-503

THE GOSPEL PARADOX

THE GOSPEL PARADOX

ROBERT JAVELET

HERDER AND HERDER

1966
HERDER AND HERDER NEW YORK
232 Madison Avenue, New York 10016

Original edition:
Les paraboles contra la loi,
Editions Saint-Paul, Paris, 1962.
This translation was made by Donald Antoine.

Nihil obstat:	Thomas J. Beary
	Censor Librorum
Imprimatur:	†Robert F. Joyce
	Bishop of Burlington
	December 23, 1965

The *Nihil obstat* and *Imprimatur* are official declarations that a book or pamphlet is considered to be free of doctrinal or moral error. No implication is contained therein that those who have granted the *Nihil obstat* and *Imprimatur* agree with the contents, opinions, or statements expressed.

Library of Congress Catalog Card Number: 66–16945
© 1966 by Herder and Herder, Incorporated
Manufactured in the United States

BT
375.2
J313

Contents

Introduction	7
The Sower	27
The Vine-Dressers	38
The Workers at the Eleventh Hour	50
The Talents	62
The Wise and Foolish Virgins	76
The Two Prodigal Sons	90
The Barren Fig Tree	116
The Good Samaritan	125
The Lost Sheep	153
The Exemplary Unjust Steward	163
The Unmerciful Servant	182
The Rich Man and Lazarus	189
The Invited	206
Conclusion	215

Introduction

THE Gospel parables are oases of freshness and simplicity, and yet they are packed with drama—the drama of Christ! They are not merely delightful moral stories said to charm Christian hearts. Certainly, from very early childhood the minds of the faithful have been filled with these living and somewhat mysterious parables in which the soul is provided a glimpse into the wisdom of Christ. They were the best weapon in catechisms against a dogmatism which naïvely defied all pedagogy. But, in a certain sense, nothing is less normal than the parables; and Christians, eager for a deeper understanding of their faith, feel annoyed with the paradoxes which are beyond them and which the eloquent elucidating of preachers does not succeed in drowning.

It is certain that the parables share in the ambiguity of revelation. The Ineffable eternally begets his Word, and in time, the Word reveals himself in holy Scripture, and even more clearly by Emmanuel. He is nothing other than the authentic transcription of the Divine Mystery. This is so. But it is still only a transcription: the infinite accessible to the finite. This realization is so perilous, however, that many witnesses or hearers of Christ refused to believe it, and St. Paul saw only annihilation in it. In

7

order to understand this heavenly message we must read the sign of God in the human life of Christ and his discourses. The pulsing vibrance revealed in his life and teaching marks the difference in levels between the Perfect and the imperfect, and it invites us to a transposition which raises up visible realities to invisible Realities. The path leads to the departure point where man is transcended, and, through ecstasy, reaches out to absolute Truth. That is, no true existential interpretation of the Bible is possible without the breath of the Holy Spirit—this same Spirit which cries out: *Abba,* Father!, and makes the Word of the Father intelligible to us.

The fact that reason, especially with regard to the parables, is utterly baffled in the face of certain doctrines, manifests their transcendence. But because Truth and Life are so closely related, we must commit ourselves to a thorough purification and sanctification process in order that we may better understand them. Without the aid of spiritual experience, their interpretation can only be words, words and merely more words! For how can one who does not love possibly understand the language of love? Though there are transpositions which lift the mind towards the object of its awareness, there are also only too many projections of noble values caught up in the mire of egotism and sensuality. The worldly man snatches at a mystical experience and he monetizes it. The politician takes possession of religion and incorporates it into his vision of a world of power. The esthete only sees the splendor of ritual in it. . . . We see, then, that it is not a question of lowering the divine to the human, but quite the opposite. Abraham left his rich fields for the wilderness that was the Promised Land. What could be more normal than that we should be out of our own element at the end of our course, and equally, what could be more normal than that the accounts of our exploration be misunderstood! The parables do not furnish our quest with a morality of equalitarian justice any more than does a moral code like that of Kant. . . . No, they are no more a code of stiff-necked virtue than is the sentimental virtue of Greuze. . . . Neither is it a question of right or of law, but of charity, the good news of Charity: God's morality, a wisdom which is folly for men when it does not scandalize them!

As we shall later see in more detail, the parable of the sower points right to the difficulty of such a teaching. The parable is not reserved to a small tribe of people, for all men have been called, but it is only made intelligible to those whose hearts have been sufficiently elevated to Christ and who know how to ascend with him to the summit of the beatitudes. . . . Besides this, a certain amount of prudence is in demand: Christ never intended casting his pearls to swine, and the mystery of the parables protects them against debasing interpretations. For on a certain plane the surpassing of the moral order by the spiritual order is interpreted as a suppression of the moral order and the authorization of worse things to follow. Now the saint practices morality, but he does so in the spirit of love and not in the mechanical living of an anonymous regulation. Moreover, it is this tendency, we believe, which, though unconsciously, has led preachers to moralize the parables, to water them down and edit them. A number of the early Christians suppressed the Gospel account of the adulteress whose sins Christ forgave because they feared that our Lord's mercy might appear the reward for sin. And yet the fact of this scandalous mercy remains. No one has got the right to sin, and all repentant sinners have the right to be forgiven. He who is forgiven more loves more, and because he loves he looks upon his sin with dread and then hastens to make reparation for it. The egotist exploits goodness; but the miracle of abundant goodness sometimes pulls a man out of his selfishness.

In our opinion, the inveterate Pharisaism of Christians is the one thing most likely to give a wrong interpretation to the parables. For the most part they remain devoted to a legalistic, mercenary, "no cash down" religion regulated by the thrust-and-parry of threats and promises. If we tell a Christian, "Love Christ, and then go out and do what you will!", would he not understand this phrase of St. Augustine as authorization for debauchery bought at the price of a bit of pious sentiment? His moral virtue, if traditionally solid, will impel him to cast off that shameful axiom. But will he reflect upon the fact that he who loves does freely and joyfully all that the Beloved wishes? Is he not distrustful of what he scornfully calls the "mystical doctrine"? He is afraid of losing his foothold, afraid of being involved in spite of himself in those situations that his reason will no longer be able to control; he mistrusts love, speaks disdainfully of it and fears it: he mocks it in order to prevent himself from submitting to the only Law which he does not desire, and in the depths of his soul he hates it. The hatred of the doctor of the Law smolders within him ready to burst into flames like wood at the foot of the stake. If the Gospel makes such an issue

10

of Pharisaism, it is because Christ's struggle against this formalistic mentality waxes hotter, for such a mentality as that is the
congenital vice of religion. When Christ teaches that his is the
religion of the Spirit and Truth, he did not mean that it is to
be celebrated in the fields or in the woods with the chirping
of birds for organ music. Rather he meant that it is the religion of
truth, and truth is not to be found in appearances, rituals, or
formulas, but in a new way of being in accordance with the
divine will—it is interior truth welling up from the Holy Spirit.

Scientific or Religious Exegesis

The parables present the essence of Christianity as opposed to
the Pharisaism of yesterday and today. The very nature of the
parables makes their inner meaning obscure to the slaves of the
Law and clear to the sons of God, but they always remain just
inside the aura of mystery so that the mind, trembling and
excited, feels transported into the spiritual. In this book the aim
of our commentaries upon the most important parables is both
to make Christ's major conflict better known and to show what
the true Evil is and what the true Virtue is for the Christian.
In light of this, then, our exegesis has no pretensions whatever
of being scientific, for we do away with that kind of scholarly
approach which tends to strangle the freedom of the spirit. Ours
is a spiritual exegesis.

In the following pages you will not find any kind of commentary which considers each thread at the bottom of a tapestry
without studying its proper relation to the surface face-work.

11

What such a commentary looks upon as absurd is of great interest: it is that which raises us up to a loftier understanding, to the rarefied but nonetheless quite real vision of the whole picture woven into the cloth, and this picture is invisible to man in his earthbound state.

But while we do respect the scholars who assure us of the authenticity of scriptural texts, who weigh and judge their phrases and words, are we obliged to risk strangling the parables to death just as literature teachers often choke out the life of poetry with their ponderous analyses? Dare we unravel all the threads of a tapestry just to repair it? And besides, is it absolutely necessary to discover whether or not a parable is more or less allegorical . . . or to find out whether we are dealing with a parabolical allegory? We grant that an allegory may be explained by direct application, each word containing a hidden meaning; or by substitution, in unravelling a series of fixed meanings, but without recalling the literal text of the metaphors; and finally by comparison: what is here . . . is there! However, we do not think that the parables are simply developed comparisons and that it is sufficient to uncover the principal lesson to bring the story to the two terms of a comparison. Such a concept—on a horizontal plane—somewhere between a tableau recounting an imaginary story or real-life event and an application giving the key to the parable—seems to us quite arbitrary and leads one to question the value of some of the story's features or scenes accordingly as they figure in the application or not. Such attempts are rather clever, but can we be certain of them? We can liken such a parabolist to a magician working with his own subjective imagination, rather than with explicit exegesis. Only here the parabolist is the Word, and how can we find difficulty in believing that even one of his words is not of infinite worth?

It is possible for us to make beautiful collections of dried, pressed, and mounted flowers. But this is nothing in comparison to actually walking among living perfumes and living colors when such flowers hint to you of beauties of which they are merely the glowing image! When we live among flowers, how our hearts are lifted up to the prime source of all beauty, to the Supreme Beauty! This is so even when we do not know their common names and individual places in botanical classifications! Does not the bee, gorging itself with pollen, have more right to wither up life than the scholar who labels and pigeonholes everything he finds? Science dries up the spirit, but love opens the soul to unbelievable horizons. And that is why we prefer not to use the scientific method in our study—particularly here where Christ himself desired so much enchantment, simplicity, and life. But we do not wish to replace science with mere moral drivel, since it is morality with which we are concerned. We are presenting to the reader not a dogmatic theology, but rather a spiritual study of intensely beautiful and enormously rich parables.

The Middle Ages invite us to this kind of method, but they were so free, so original, that we can only be inspired by them and not imitate them. The spiritual writers of the twelfth century distinguished three levels of awareness in man. Here the word "level" is improper, for we are concerned with a dynamic attitude of the spirit. Let it suffice to call them "moments" of awareness analogous to a magnet's "moment of attraction." Man is "carnal" if his attention is fixed to the sensible world. He is "rational" or spiritual (pneumatic) according to whether he is bound to the world of essence—or to the divine world. The senses equate him with the sensible, and reason with the world of ideas (viewed concretely—for we must distinguish this reasoning from abstract reasoning). Intelligence reads into the essences of beings—and into God as well. It is the intuition of beings in their relation to God; it is the loving awareness, without words or ideas, of the divine pleroma . . . and it is this awareness whose mission it is to penetrate the holy Scriptures which reveal this divine world. An Abelard would praise human reason which can only produce a certain theology when it prescinds from the gifts of faith. But he is mistaken if he pretends to a living knowledge of the divine. Understanding, enlightened by charity, is the only "eye" capable of searching out the secrets of heaven. Through spirituality, and with God's grace, man is transcended and approaches an understanding of contemplation. When the mystery, although ineffable, is perceived, the understanding becomes "mystical" through the grace of God. Provided that the carnal or rational minds are not closed in upon themselves, and provided that they are at least susceptible to divine influence, then the understanding is apt to speak to them of the divine, apt to communicate it to them with words and ideas, and it is apt to perceive the logic.

There are, then, three ways in which we may consider the biblical message if we are to draw its teaching out. They are the literal or historical sense, the allegorical sense—depending on the gift of faith—which searches out the Christian "ideas," and lastly, the tropological sense which concerns the interior life, the nourishment of the soul by the Word. The anagogical sense, called the fourth sense, is nothing other than the movement of the spirit lifting the carnal to the spiritual which, literally, by meditation on the ideas is raised up to an understanding of the divine mysteries.

Moreover, the value accorded to the spiritual explains that the authors admitted the multiplicity of tropological meanings, while they defended the unity of the literal sense. The more the sense is elevated, the richer and more polyvalent it becomes. The soul takes the nectar suitable to it. And we cannot help but thinking that the nectar it chooses has been secreted by the soul itself. We get the impression of being in a spiritual subjectivism. For our part, we think that this imaginative juggling of writings to meet different ends and with the most varied interpretations, is what we shall call the "mystical sense." The anagogical approach only seeks out the meaning God intended to give, and the higher we ascend, the more unification there is, for the fewer words and ideas there are, the nearer we draw to the eternal Silence, the divine *Urgrund*. But when we are committed to the downward path of theophanies, revelation becomes increasingly many-sided, as the Letter to the Hebrews points out. Spiritual writers of the twelfth century, thoroughly imbued in "spiritual reading" and well grounded in the Old and New Testaments—when they wished to communicate what they perceived of the divine mysteries, they made use of Biblical expressions. It seemed to them that there was no better vocabulary, and moreover the holy

15

images and comparisons other than those offered them in the sacred texts were so assimilated in their minds that this knowledge mingled in with all other branches.

Thus we can see that a man such as Richard of St. Victor, commentating upon the text of Isaiah, "*Custos, quid de nocte?*" ("Watchman, what of the night?"), was immediately reminded of an etymological factor: he recalled that "Samaritan" means "watchman." He developed an explanation of the parable with the aid of his principal theme:

> Temptation by the devil brings on the night; divine inspiration brings the day. Each time we sin, either through ignorance or malice, we are cast into darkness; then we must appeal to our Samaritan. Watchman, what of the night? . . . Who is this watchman to whom we cry out during the night, if he is not the Samaritan who took pity on the man, fallen into the hands of thieves. (*PL* 196, 1008)

A true interpretation of this parable is of little importance. The parable serves to dress up a real truth which the spiritual writer wanted to make better known. Had he wanted to distinguish the promise of pardon from the promise of grace and the promise of glory, corresponding to the purgative, illuminative, and unitive ways of the spiritual life, he would at once have noticed there is no better illustration than the three parables involving oil. This is the way he interprets the oil with which the Samaritan dressed the man's wounds, the oil with which the unfaithful steward paid his debt, and the extra supply of oil of the wise virgins. The interpretation can be objective. But that is not Richard's problem, who would use, had he needed to, some other symbolism according to his need at the moment.

16

One commentary, in particular, reveals the fundamental problem of the teaching of the spiritual life. It is when the personages of the parable are translated into sentiment, into psychological states of the soul considered in its unity. It is no longer a question of good and evil, but of virtue and vice in the same individual.

The straightforwardness of the last promise [Richard wrote of the parable of the workers at the eleventh hour] is the symbol of the integrity of the true and sovereign perfection promised to the workers in the Lord's vineyard. This payment is only accorded at the end of day after the work has been completed. The Lord's vineyard is man's conscience; it is the choice vineyard in which the Lord has planted every seed of truth. In order to cultivate this vineyard, the Lord goes out of it when he has made his will known through an interior aspiration. The Lord's coming out of the vineyard is its manifestation. The reiteration of this exitus is the increase of knowledge. There are as many manifestations as there are excursions from the vineyard. The differences in the hours represent various degrees of progress. That is why throughout the course of the day and the succession of hours, the Lord comes and goes, since divine knowledge increases according to the progress of perfection and the promotion of virtues. The laborers in the vineyard represent thoughts and feelings. Workers of this kind have to cultivate the vineyard because both must sweat to purify the conscience. The one must toil to find truth; the other must labor to practice virtue. The first have got to cut away immorality and get rid of whatever is opposed to good morals. The task of the former is to correct their faults, and the job of the latter is the mortification of vices. At daybreak, and at the third, sixth, ninth, and eleventh hours, men are brought into the vineyard to sweat and toil. The sunlight first appears in the early morning hours; at the third hour the sun is usually shining brightly; but at the sixth hour it is scorchingly hot; at the ninth hour, the sun begins its downward plunge; and at the eleventh hour the light and heat are gradually decreasing. But what is the beginning of the day if not the illumination of truth, and what is the gradual increase of the heat if not the acceptance of goodness? The gentle warmth of the sun is the fervor of dilection. Its cooling is the hatred of vanity. What else can the approach of nightfall with its decreasing light and heat signify but the repression of carnal desire, or even the weakening of carnal prudence? That is why daybreak is the discernment of good and evil; the third hour the desire for true good, noon the desire of supreme good, the ninth hour disgust of false goods, and the eleventh hour hatred of, and flight from, true evil. The more the appetites and other human senses are restricted to what is just, the more they receive the reward of retribution and the form of perfection. They are drawing near to the frankness of integrity. In fact, all perceive that the promised money at the end of the day is nothing other than the obtaining at last of a form of perfection in all our senses.

When the time of retribution is at hand, when the denarius of perfection is given as recompense to the Lord's workmen, no more will be given to desire than to counsel, and nothing less to thought than to feeling. That is why the last receive the same denarius as those who first came to work. But what is meant by the laborer who began work at daybreak, was at last paid and was rebuked with these words: "Take what is yours and go! . . . Or are you envious because I am generous?" Who would toil to the very point of exhaustion for purity of heart and would wear himself out tilling the vineyard if his conscience did not torment him? That is why the first laborer in the vineyard signifies thought, the accuser of the conscience. This laborer's envy is all the more loathsome to us because God will be kind and generous to us. This workman's labor is not finished as long as the least imperfection subsists and as long as the man's whole being is not totally transformed and made suitable to receive the reward of perfection. But after he has been paid, let him take what is his and go: he will not find anything to reproach in justice. Oh, what a perfection of knowledge and fulfillment of virtue there will be then! (*PL* 196, 1142)

In this introduction we have been determined to translate this curious, subtle, and profound explanation of a difficult parable.

It only lacks some further development. The text suffices, it seems to us, to illustrate what the spiritual exegesis of the Middle Ages is like, and how it differs from modern exegesis. At least it has the merit of being concrete and vibrant; it inspires us to fervent, clear-sighted sentiments which we may take with us on our spiritual journey. It manifests a rare feeling of introspection and psychological analysis. How can we help but admire Richard's ability to use details from the parable account to work out a description of the stages of spiritual growth which leads to full integrity or perfection to such a point that we are tempted to think it was this exegesis of the parable that suggested the spiritual description in the first place. It is our opinion that sometimes there are actually instances where one does react upon the other. It is something like a poetical rhyme: the rhyme being determined by what preceded it, and its necessity sometimes quickens unexpected imageries in the mind. Sometimes it is quite like an embarrassing trick, and at other times it is as joyful as the face of a laughing sprite. It is hardly necessary to add that, while admiring the inventive genius and insight of the spiritual writer whose selection we have chosen, accustomed as we are to a modern rigorousness we cannot consent to the flagrantly subjective character and occasionally too clever creative ability of such commentaries. But, at all costs, we have got to retain their clearly spiritual character.

The Fathers of the Church present us with effective examples of less subjective commentaries, such as those of St. Gregory. So, when he writes on the parable of the wedding guest: A king made a great banquet and invited very many people. . . , St. Gregory changes the earthly feast into a spiritual banquet:

There is quite a difference between the delicacies of the body and those of the heart. The lack of bodily delights enkindles powerful desires in the body; but when, in fact, desire is glutted, they are quickly satiated, even to the point of disgusting the one who indulged in them. Spiritual delicacies, on the contrary, are not tempting when they are lacking; but they provoke desire when they are possessed. He who feeds upon spiritual delicacies is all the more hungry for making them his nourishment, than is he who is hungry for them. (Homily 36, *In Evang.*)

He follows this up with some interesting speculations on the appetite and taste for the spiritual to the extent that the parable is obscured. But his most obvious mistake is slipping into dogmatic allegory, usually based upon the symbolism of numbers. Thus there are, he says, five virgins because man has five senses. The number two connotes human and divine nature, and so on. A particularly clear-cut example of theological tendency is the parable of the wedding feast. Right from the outset we are in a more objective and less personalistic world.

The kingdom of heaven is the Church of the just; indeed, their hearts aspire to nothing worldly, but sigh for loftier things: the Lord already reigns within them as he rules in heaven. We say then: the kingdom of heaven is like unto a man who prepared a wedding feast for his son. Already your charity comprehends [*intelligit*] who this King is, the Father of a Son who is King; certainly, it is he of whom the Psalmist sings, "Oh God, with your judgment endow the King and with your justice the King's son!" He made a wedding feast for his son. Truly, God the Father made a wedding feast for his Son when he joined his Son to human nature in the Virgin's womb. . . . But the nuptial union is usually the action of two persons. Let us cast that idea from our minds. Let us not believe that the God-man, our Redeemer, is the union of two persons. Of course, we say he exists in and with two natures, but it would be sacrilegious to believe that he is composed of two persons. Beware of that concept!

20

It is clearer to imagine, and truer to say, that by the wedding feast which the Father prepared for his Son the King, he meant that by the incarnation, the Father has associated the holy Church to his Son. (Homily 38, *In Evang.*)

We do not think that a profound study has ever been made on the subject of the parables according to the Fathers. The remarkable thing of their exegesis is the anagogical tendency. With their obvious previous acquaintance, they depart from the text, but they do so in order to rise up to an exact interpretation of the Gospel text. The ideas in the back of their heads deviate from an ascension which promises to be objective. And suddenly they arrive at moral proliferation. Sometimes their considerations are historical and have the advantage of not ignoring the Church from the outset. But we do not find, as in the Middle Ages, the supple utilization of the texts by a mind which incorporates them into the spiritual doctrine whose experience it desires to communicate.

In our opinion, the succinct commentary of St. Jerome on the "unfaithful steward" is the norm to follow. He doubtlessly, soon afterwards, slips into the natural level and gets himself all entangled when he considers the use of riches; but before that, his was a genuine example of anagogical spiritual exegesis.

If, therefore, the dispenser of the mammon of iniquity is commended by the voice of his Lord, because he has acquired justification, then thanks be to him who is unjust; if in spite of his loss the Lord praises the steward's prudence, though he indeed acted fraudulently against his Lord, but wisely for himself; how much more will Christ, who cannot tolerate any wrong and who is prompt in mercy, praise his disciples if they show mercy to those who will be indebted to them? (Epistle 121, *Ad Algasiam,* 9–6. PL 22, 1019)

21

There we find that upward tendency and spiritual expression which we think are characteristic of a true exegesis of parables.

As our commentary on this same parable will show, this method which we have made thorough use of will appear all the more clearly to react against the evil tendency that results from too many acrobatical commentaries. To be sure, as we find with the beatitudes, more than properly fixed dogma, the spiritual is the most important aspect of the parables. We say *spiritual*, for it is not a question of human morality, but of the living Law of God offered to the sons of God. It cannot be the question of a wise use of earthly goods, nor of almsgiving . . . any more than the parable of the royal wedding feast teaches the protocol of wearing the proper garments, or the parable of the sower recommends sowing only on good land, or the parable of the mustard seed being told to amaze horticulturists on the astonishing growth of the mustard seed.

When we come across worldly things in a parable, we must change them into spiritual goods and then stay constantly on that plane. It does no good to eliminate a problem brought up in a parable by simplifying and reducing it to a facile solution. Perhaps to omit even the most insignificant detail is to miss the point. Anyhow, the obstacle permits that leap, that transcendence, just as a diving board gives added impetus to a more powerful dive. Those things which astonish and scandalize are important. The meaning of the mystery is the problem. Because we have been nourished with Christian thought and paradoxes, it is easier for us to understand what their "sesame" is. The intuition of the departure, more exactly the premonition that it

22

was Christ's intention to reveal a spiritual order of charity, of absolute exigency and full pardon against a Pharisaical order of pseudo-equinanimity characteristic of what has been called a static religion or closed society, this premonition which distinguished the mystic of the Gospel in these familiar stories told in Galilee, was able to guide and has certainly aided research, but has not dominated or tyrannized it. What had been uncovered in barely apparent filigree is found confirmed by a deeper meditation which benefited from earlier readings, but which is simply brought about by the confrontation of the soul with the sacred text.

Moreover, is not the secret of the method in the Gospel itself, when we find there a succinct commentary on it, but suggestive of the parables of the sower or of the weeds? It appears Christ used no other method than the transposition of all parable content to the spiritual level where a new logic appears—which is not perplexing provided we admit the laws of love. The transposition being quite simple and word for word, it can be supposed that at the base of the story's plan there is usually something abnormal—which arouses interest . . . provided we are not exasperated if our minds are of a modernistic or scientistic bent.

In any case, it is a question of "religious" fables from which we derive a religious lesson that alone matters—in the same way as we draw out a moral lesson from Aesop's fables. The narrative is of value not insofar as the story is true, but insofar as the transposition is spiritual. The parable is not a little drama of good or bad consequences which develop a thought useful to daily living. It should rather be classed among the myths; but the dogmatic is beyond the myths; and beyond the parable is the spiritual life—the life of God to which man is called to live in him and by his grace.

Certainly, we do not contribute anything totally new and definitive. The parables are so full of the sun that their reading has always rewarded Christians with a marvelous abundance of rays of light. But if, in an age where the letter takes precedence over the spirit, we invite modern exegesis, without losing its science, to understand that the traditional exegesis, in spite of its shortcomings or its fantasies, at least had a soul and knew how to communicate it, then this exegetical spiritual essay will not have been in vain.

It is not our purpose here to pass all the parables in review, but merely those of most interest because they are most controversial. We have written whatever each one inspired us to write, giving several a particular emphasis—and without being afraid of the unevenness of the chapters! Each commentary is a whole unit in itself and each sets its own tone. The parable themes clash with, and converge against, the Law, and therefore certain repetitions are inevitable: but they will have the advantage of driving the point home, of firmly imprinting the basic theme of this book. If the parables have an indisputable unity, they also offer a supple harmonical diversity, which, without being too arbitrary about it, allows us to treat them according to the rhythmical logic of their teachings, so that we may construct a complete symphony out of the whole.

We have chosen the parable of the *sower* first because Christ

24

confronts the Law and proclaims charity: he sows the spiritual revolution. The parable of the *vine-dressers* shows what it costs to be prophets of the Good News. Yet every soul must answer the call which summons him to his mission; he must set out promptly at the hour God selects; this call and its response are personal, in the order of this love which does not consider itself, neither does it weigh and measure, nor does it split up. This doctrine is made vivid in the parable of the *workers at the eleventh hour*. The parable of the *talents* shows that the apostle's reward is a new obligation, requiring added self-sacrifice. He who conforms to this law of generosity is wise: so we have the parable of the *wise and foolish virgins*.

The parables of the *two prodigal sons* and the *barren fig tree* teach us the need to cleanse our hearts from all Pharisaism. The love of God and neighbor is the law of the Christian heart—not two loves, but one: the *good Samaritan* declares it. This charity which binds the whole Christian community is realized in examining the parable of the *lost sheep*. We must forgive as God does, in the name of God: that is the lesson of the *unjust steward*, emphasized by the lot of the *unmerciful servant*. The dramatic fate of those who do not love is unfolded in the parables of the *rich man and Lazarus* and the *invited*. Our conclusion with the parable of the *weeds* recalls the scandal of evil in this world and the necessity of patience as a spiritual force—to keep us from ending up the same way as the Rich Man and the supper guests. The conclusion with the parable of the *weeds* recalls the *publican*. In this way we approach the divine life in communion with all who slake their thirst at the same waters and are the faithful branches of the *True Vine*. Finally, since we are also concerned with our brothers, mankind, each one of us learns how to obtain the Bread of Salvation for them from the *importunate friend*. We all have got to ask our heavenly Father unceasingly for love.

The Sower

MATTHEW 13, 1–23
MARK 4, 1–20
LUKE 8, 4–15

WE shall discuss the parable of the sower first because Christ himself has provided us with the key to it. Every word of Christ is inexhaustible and his commentary is a treasure house for all who love his word and desire to reap the hundredfold harvest.

When our Lord explained the meaning of this parable to the apostles, it seemed so evident as to be trite. We encounter it in our first year of catechism class and often we leave it behind there. Had there been no opposition among the people in the crowd "who do not understand," and had the apostles not been admitted to a special light, had there not been this problem of the obscuring use of enigmas and esoterism, the exegetes would no longer discuss the sower. But because Christ did explain this parable they know that he is the Word, the Master (Rabbi, Teacher, the Divine Pedagogue), and they know that the seed is nothing less than his thought, his Gospel preached, and so filled with potential for every heart according to the welcome reserved there for it.

Scholarly Exegesis

Here is a sower who sows his grain carelessly—on the wayside, on rocks and among thorns—as well as on good earth. Why such an example? Why does the Messiah appear as a clumsy, slow-witted farmer? Deliberately? They who obstinately try to rationalize the follies of those whom they love, immerse themselves in the study of geography, natural sciences, georgics, archeology, so that through their effort they may be able to reconstruct history—but they starch with their learned erudition everything wonderful, and turn out statements like this: "The Palestinian fellah* sows just as he pleases," or: "Jesus, seated in a boat, saw a fellah at a distance sowing regardless of where!" And so amazed are they that the Lord selected this extravaganza to emphasize his way of preaching the kingdom of heaven, that these well-intentioned savants return to their first declaration: "It was perfectly normal; everyone found it natural. In those days it was expected of a fellah to sow carelessly. Jesus, who conformed to traditions . . . so as not to conflict with the mental habits and experiences of his listeners . . . took his example such as it appeared in its sublime historical truth." Having said this much, the well-meaning exegete adds: "Otherwise he would not attach an exaggerated importance to certain details. There is a backdrop to the parable, there are little facts recounted in order to enliven, to animate the narrative . . . but they have

* "Fellah"—a peasant.

28

no important bearing on the exegesis itself. So when we encounter these passages which impede us, we set them aside and
apply another methodology to them. Of course, it is not easy
to distinguish between the important Gospel passages and the
less important, but we are intelligent, and reason has not been
accorded to us exegetes in vain. When our reason does not
understand the meaning, it is an evident sign that it is incomprehensible. . . ." Scholars and exegetes argue in this manner
quite certain of their wisdom, and categorize the folly of the
sower into the filing cabinets of history or as Hebraic-Aramaic
figurative literary styles. The unkind scholars and exegetes who
lean somewhat in either direction, but whose feelings are luke-
warm, gloss over the sacred text: "The fellah," they say, "is
only a bit foolish [the degree of his foolishness depending on
the subjective kindness of the critic]; for he sows the good earth
by the handful, but he measures the seed for the wayside, the
brambles, and the rocks." Oh, what wisdom! We thank heaven
we do not know any truly malevolent scholars and exegetes: the
unkind are supportable, but the malevolent would cut holes in
the sower's seedbag.

No, the Gospel sower is not a classic fool made to seem
normal in the historicity of his folly, nor is he a calculating fool,
a cold-blooded fool, any more than he is a clumsy man, a
lamentable person, a newcomer to the art of sowing a field, a
thoughtless good-natured man, an ignoramus confusing the roadside for the field (and on that we should have a great deal to
say, for there were no roads by the fields—they are still not yet
tarred). The evangelist did not say there was a strong wind on
that particular day, a wind scattering the seeds here and there.

Nor did he say the sower was unaware of his strength on that morning when he threw his seeds too far. And in addition, he did not say that this improvident man was a wastrel and scattered the seed all over the place.

Universal Charity

Christ did know what he was about in telling the story of the sower who scattered his grain everywhere—and not aimlessly—even in those places where one does not usually sow. Christ foresaw that his parable would provoke negative reactions, a failure to understand on the part of the common people who heard his words, because he all of a sudden had revealed to them his kingdom where man's wisdom is folly, and his folly is wisdom.

The great sower is the Father. Everything that is, lives, and thinks comes from him. God "makes his sun to rise on the good and the evil, and sends rain on the just and the unjust."[1] He sows his creative and salvific Word everywhere. Because creation is multiform, he also permitted vast areas of rock-hard soil which do not support life, and there next to freedom it was sowed, where there are untroubled and fertile lands opened to grace through the glistening wounds of long furrows. The sower does not walk that ground alone, for there stalks over this land that ragged soldiery of anxieties and earthly desires, that restlessness of humanity which seeks its own happiness and passes by trampling the earth without having sowed it. In these rocky places where some fertile clumps of soil are all but lost among

[1] Mt. 5, 45.

the innumerable stones holding back the furrowing blade of the plough, the sower will only find thorns where the ground is open to nothing but selfishness and passions, at first flattering, and eventually evil and cruel.

God's goodness created everything in his Word and in the Spirit. When mankind does not act as God would desire, it does not follow that he abandons it. God never ceases replanting, and this parable tells of the sowing of the redemptive Word—the re-creation of the world. But still, divine generosity does not come to nothing because of hardened waysides, stones, and thorns. The Father who created everything still wants to save everything. From him all things come into being, and he loves all things infinitely. The Father remains with us in spite of our ingratitude. He is even Father to his prodigal children. The magnificence of divine charity is this: It takes exception to no one, it never shuts itself off from anyone, and it never seeks vengence. The wicked are never forgotten. Heavenly favors descend upon them just as upon the good, and they do so with the reckless abandon of a love which knows no bounds! And yet in this truth lies their awesome responsibility.

The Father sows and Jesus is the seed, the only living seed who is communicated in a multitude of words like the communion hosts which are really a single bread. He who chooses to sow God's thought like the Father sows, will not be concerned with fertile grounds only, that is, with faithful souls in the state of grace, those well-disposed creatures ready to respond to love. He sows, even without a reasonable hope, to arouse other generous hearts capable of sowing in their turn, so that eventually there will be reward for all, possibility for all, and hope for all. If some are not saved, that is their affair. The spirit of evil dwelling in them will carry off the seed unable to penetrate into a heart preoccupied by anything but God. The seed will perhaps at first find some fault on which to germinate, but among those who withdraw into themselves, it will soon wither away. The ego, prisoner of itself, will not be set free from its monstrous self-adoration, it will not spring up as a verdant offering to others. Among other people, in spite of some pure forces, the conflict of interests and sensual delights will savagely smother any joyful hopes for a better world. Free men may freely deliver themselves up to be slaves of evil, just as they may open their hearts to charity. But love sets no boundaries, it is limitless, non-calculating, it is the same as wisdom: love, the gift of folly.

The type of seed makes the difference: it is sacrificed. If its sacrifice takes root, what joy there is! But, if it is lost, if conquered by the Evil One, what a tragedy! What Christ does is good. Some received him, others drove him away, sold and crucified him. God's message is neither words nor doctrine, but a love which makes loving possible. It is a life which makes living possible. If the Word fails, it dies, and whoever refuses it dies as well, but it is not the same kind of death. When will men understand that heaven is the foster mother of the earth? When will they learn that heavenly nourishment is absolutely necessary for existence? The dried ear of wheat does not live. The living ear produces life. Man is this ear of wheat. He is not simply fed from the earth, but from every rich and life-giving word coming from the mouth of God—the word which expresses love's folly. The living speak with the word of God. The dead fall silent, and in the darkness of the silence the word becomes the anguished cry of the One who died with love for all, for all including his enemies and those who did not know what they were doing![2] In this way the Word of God speaks to all creation: "Greater love than this no one has, that he lay down his life for his friends!"[3]

So it is that the parable clears up the mystery of divine Charity, the mystery of redemption for all mankind, and not just for a select few. That all are not saved proves the freedom of creatures (love does not constrain), and it points out the implacable hardness in which, being filled up with themselves or with other false gods, they are frozen solid. God gives, sows his Word for all to harvest: such is his objective. The goal is not always reached—and this is the tragedy of salvation.

The Parable and Teaching of Christ

We see that the parable clears up those disputes arising from Christ's teaching: Does God speak so as not to be understood, to "dull the hearts" of a rejected people predestined to damnation? Does God keep a select minority for himself to whom—with a scandalous preference—he confides the secrets of life, the seed of salvation? How can we imagine such things as these? And was it not necessary that the parable of love for all shine light onto the meanings that Christ intended, before and after the explanation of the narrative—these meanings which are surrounded with a marvelous light? For each parable is a sun, a ray at least, that dazzles and illumines as is normal when the absolute enters

[2] Lk. 23, 34.
[3] Jn. 15, 13.

into contact with the relative, the divine with the human. It is because the parable conveys a sense of mystery that it is the revealing sign of what surpasses our reason and opens our understanding to the Mystery. All the mystics know from experience what is in it. The understanding of a parable supposes a mind which is not closed off, unreceptive, by reason, a mind capable of understanding love—a fertile ground for this seed which is light and darkness as God in his creation. If God were rational light, he would be like us and would be our plaything; we would use him as technicians use theories and laws. God truly wishes to communicate himself to us, but his obscurity discloses his transcendence, the infinite eminence of his Truth.

Having said this much, let us re-read the Gospel account. Jesus, in telling his little parable of the sower, concludes: "He who has ears, let him hear!"[4] The whole thing is to be able to hear just as it is to be a fertile ground. Then the apostles came near him and asked, "Why do you speak to them in parables?" He answers, "To you it is given to know the mysteries of the kingdom of heaven, but to them it is not given. For to him who has shall be given, and he shall have abundance; but from him who does not have, even that which he has shall be taken away. This is why I speak to them in parables, because seeing they do not see, and hearing they do not hear, neither do they understand."[5] Jesus sees the terrible fulfillment of Isaiah's prophecy: "Hearing you will hear, but not understand; and seeing you will see, but not perceive. For the heart of this people has been hardened, and with their ears they have been hard of hearing,

[4] Mt. 13, 9.
[5] Mt. 13, 13.

and their eyes they have closed; lest at any time they see with their eyes, and hear with their ears, and understand with their mind, and be converted and I heal them."[6]

Jesus continues: "But blessed are your eyes, for they see; and your ears, for they hear."[7] He then explains his parable: "Hear, therefore, the parable of the sower. When anyone hears the word of the kingdom, but does not understand it, the wicked one comes and snatches away what has been sown in his heart. . . ."[8]

Christ's first words combine with and seem to validate Jansenistic interpretations: a gloomy predestination! But the prophecy of Isaiah shows the true reason accounting for the diabolical incomprehension of those who prefer not to be restored to spiritual health. They wish not to understand so they will not have to change, so as not to find their souls once again made pure by the Son of God. That is why—the parable makes it clear—the word of salvation, the seed of grace and life, is ravished by the Prince of Darkness. This is what we make known: the suffering of him who has given everything for all people and whose sacrifice is vain for some people, on account of the pride within their hearts. It is not enough to have ears: God has given to everyone the means to hear. It is not enough that there be the Word: Jesus Christ who is God gave it to all. It does not even suffice to hear the Word: it is not enough that the evangelical message be made known, be made apparent, even scientifically apparent, by striking erudition. The Scribes of the Law all heard the Lord; their ears resounded to the sound of

[6] Is. 6, 9–10; Mt. 13, 14–15.
[7] Mt. 13, 16.
[8] Mt. 13, 18–19.

his voice and their brains resounded to his thought! But they did not understand. In order to understand, freshly tilled soil is imperative, that is, an open heart, capable of loving, capable by itself to quicken love, at the appeal of infinite Charity. The disciples, those who followed Jesus, were those who understood: they loved! That is why our Lord explained what they—like the rest of the crowd—had heard. The whole thing is grace! Behind those words which were uttered was the Person of Christ who penetrated the words to the very depths of their being, in a moving gentleness, in a divine understanding of the prodigality of the eternal Sower. It makes no difference who can take within himself deep into the infatuated void of his mind this word which is the personal Voice of the Father, so long as he is not wrapped up in himself and the world and his own vices. To understand is to communicate, and then growth begins, life shines with merits, and the soul becomes an immense harvest to which the hungry are invited.

Theological knowledge is not necessarily given to the disciples, to those who love, but rather the knowledge of the kingdom of heaven is theirs, a knowledge which is a gift and a superabundance of gift, for this gift is not limited to a distant participation in the Light of God, but to the deification itself. Perfect understanding or knowledge is in fact identification. For the creature who, even assumed, remains such, there is no identification strictly speaking, but rather an inexpressible union which is the unity of mind: "I shall know even as I have been known!"[9] He who believes a truth with all his might is inevitably transformed by it; it is not he who understands the truth, but the truth takes

[9] 1 Cor. 13, 12.

36

a hold on him, it flares up within him and breaks through his boundaries. Fertile soil is opened up and the ear of wheat rises up to meet the sky. . . .

The others, "seeing they do not see, and hearing they do not hear, neither do they understand." Truth slips past them. They are closed to it, hostile. They reduce everything to their own form, their own interest; they refuse the parable because of its margin of mystery, because of its corona of divinity. Little minds never admit what surpasses them. Locked in with themselves and in this world of appearances, they devote themselves to nothingness and eternal death. They were rational, but too feeble to have understanding. From now on, not only will they not have the understanding of God which they have rejected—this understanding which is the mystical union with God: beatitude—but their reason itself reels and founders in the twilight world. Without God and without the Saviour, the world has no meaning, the world is absurd . . . reason no longer recognizes itself and stumbles about in the chaos of despair. "The fool says in his heart, 'there is no God.' "[10] There is no direction, there is only a frightening whorl in the chasm of nothingness which sucks up the unbelievers, those incapable of loving and those who can no longer hope. Is not this the modern world of atheistic existentialists? Hell on earth!

But the Father sows always and everywhere. "Do not harden your hearts, call upon the Invitatory of Penitence. Do not await the death of the seed."

[10] Ps. 13, 1.

The Vine-Dressers

LUKE 20, 9–19

ISAIAH 5, 1–7

THIS parable is polemical and prophetical. It clearly joins forces in the struggle against the Pharisaism of the Law. The Scribes and high priests well understood "that he had aimed this parable at them."[1]

In it we find an historical interpretation without an anagogical transposition: real characters supplant the fictitious on the same level. By this verbal allusion the past is told and the future predicted.

The owner, representing God, has a vineyard—the Chosen People: Israel. He sends his servants—the prophets—to gather his share of the grape harvest. (At this point commentators fall silent about what the fruits are, though some suggest many kinds.) The prophets are shamefully treated: beaten, stoned, killed. The vine-grower's son, Christ, is killed outside the vineyard at the gates of Jerusalem. The vine-dressers, who represent the unfaithful Jews, are punished, being slaughtered in the year 70 A.D.

[1] Lk. 20, 19.

38

by Titus. (The precision which reduces the curse to a local and earthly disaster in which the Jews converted to Christ certainly perished, seems to us the sign of interpretive error.) Finally, the vineyard was handed over to some other people, the pagans, who formed the Church and delivered up the harvest to God at the proper time.

We believe that if we studied this parable in the light of traditional exegesis, we would not be doing any justice to it. It is our conviction that it is always necessary, even here, to transpose it to a superior level.

The anecdotal history of the difficulties facing the Chosen People and the messengers of the Most High must give place to history such as it takes place in God, and this is what we call the divine transcendent economy. We are not concerned here with an ideal history like that of the Hegelian dialectics; rather our objective is a spiritual history which transcends both time and space, where charity is at grips with man's revolt and characterized by the redemption—with everything prefiguring and preparing it.

History of a Soul

This history stands out against every man's destiny, and each soul in its history sums up the spiritual drama of salvation. Here we shall offer an analogous exegesis of this parable, as we have adopted for all the rest. After the history of a soul, we shall observe how this conflict between the Law and Love extends to the history of humanity.

God loves every soul as a vine of election; he gives it a vocation to produce fruit, to be alive and charitable. That is why he hedges it in, digs a wine press there, builds a tower; that is, he protects it with vigilance, sets up its boundaries which are the rules of wisdom, but which especially separate it, making it distinguishable from the fallow land, cutting it off from encroaching weeds. He uses every means at his disposal to cultivate and better harvest it.

This harvest, the work of grace—the divine intervention which gives it ground and plants—and the natural activity of instincts and faculties of man—the vine-dressers—is not, however, destined for man alone, to please the senses, the saturation of egotism. Man does not have the right to say, "I have worked for myself, for myself alone. The entire harvest belongs to me. Who is this God who would give me everything and to whom I must give back something? I don't see it . . . don't understand it." We can taste the transcription of the separation of God, his apparent absence. We live and struggle through existence as though everything depended on us and us alone. God remains invisible, at a noteworthy distance, and now and then he sends visitors! They are the messengers of Charity, they are secret invitations in our hearts, appeals to share with gratitude in the bottomless love of God, in his essential generosity. We must understand that each soul is imminently dependent on the love of God the Creator, and its absolute duty is to answer this love with love. When we deal with a loving God, the obligation cannot be forced: he requests and begs a free response rising out of our hearts, but it is no less a duty. In short, woe to him who shirks this responsibility! By his own actions he condemns himself.

The egocentricity of instincts and the mind mauls and kills

the good inspirations which suggest: "Keep for yourself what is useful of the goods God has given you and which you have increased, in order to do what must be done here below on earth; but let it be your will to give back to God the love due him, to return to him whatever you can, as if you would give your life to your Creator!" Egotism does not even have pity to offer the supreme Mendicant, the Son sent to soften hardened hearts: "This vain wisdom, this formalistic piety, or these voracious appetites will respect my Son! They will yield before such a love!" But the Saviour's intention and his bloodied grace which weeps at the gate of the soul, but the perfect charity which has done all things, collide into the grim wall of refusal. The soul, filled with itself, madly tortures this disquieting love it dreads which arouses remorse, awakens repentance, opens up to the generosity of love. Mysteriously caked in the sins of the world, the soul crucifies and kills in itself the sons of God. "His blood be on us and on our children!"[2] it cries out exasperated at the great crowd coming, from all ages, to this praetorium where craven selfishness condemns God to death!

The soul kills the God of love within it, for it knows that with him it must give and even be given. Now it wants to buy up divine power with the wealth of the heir. God made man has come to it; it wants to become this man who is God. Sin always boldly makes this assertion. When St. Michael the faithful archangel exclaims in his name: "Who is like unto God?", Lucifer, the unfaithful one, tempts, saying, "You will be like God!"[3] The idolatrous humanism which centers all things to itself—had it

[2] Mt. 27, 25.
[3] Gen. 3, 5.

41

the pious voracity of mercenary religions, would do the same even with God.

This humanity refuses to give to the Creator what is owed him, even if the Creator is the countenance of love.

The man who wants to be his own god, who, like Nietzsche's Superman, denounces mercy as the "weakness" of love, is incapable of looking within himself to discover the creative source of his existence in the silence of the depths of his being, and he is further incapable of reaching the archetypal Word who is the junction of the finite to the infinite. Because he refuses to love, he goes out of himself, is dispersed in the many, debases the image of God written in him, and ruins the eternal treasure over which he pretends to be the only master.

"The vine-dressers throw the Son of God out of the vineyard and there they kill him. . . ." But God makes the guilty ones "perish wretchedly." Our being is only a reflection of his being, and if God's image is destroyed in us, we are nothing. Without God, without our real "self," we are less than nothing. The rejection of God is man's failure. It seems that all rejected love turns against the walled-in heart, and its dazzling flame of paradise becomes destroying hell fire.

Certainly, it is a terrible tragedy for love that the vine-dressers sacrifice its messengers, that man refuses God who comes to him. But they who respond to grace give the increase to the divine gifts for God himself, the only benefactor, and the only "owner of the vineyard," who gives them the power of loving, with the freedom to blaspheme and hate him. Man's dependence on God is his truth and grandeur. If we decide to love, then we resemble the image of God, and by the gift of grace, we become like God.

The only way accorded man to become like God is freely to give part of the harvest back to God. To love, to give by loving, when we could keep it all, is in a way to create as God has created, making us able to speak with him and being the principle with him for the communion of love which is the paradise of charity.

History of Humanity

We must now give complete extension to our exegesis. The vineyard is the soul's to harvest; it must evangelize all humanity. The vine-dresser is the prototype of the man accountable for his brothers. Every man is born to be a prophet[4] or an apostle: his interior fire is given him to make it shine forth.[5] He is a fallen apostle if he gathers up for himself the profit and the glory, if he exalts his personality, and, hidden in the light of God, adores himself. How they present religion as "their" religion and make the disciples of God "their" disciples, attached to "their" small ideas, to "their" little passions![6] How they fall short of the mission which consists in self-abnegation, where the apostle must be effaced without winning either the love or the admiration of men, diminishing himself in order that God alone might increase, as did John the Baptist.[7] To reduce God to one's "self" is still to kill him in the self and in souls duped by the vain emptiness they admired. This inveiglement of the divine is cer-

[4] The prophet speaks "in the name of God." Occasionally, he foretells the future. But it is not the essence of his mission.

[5] Mt. 5, 14–16.

[6] 1 Cor. 3, 4–5.

[7] Jn. 3, 30.

tainly demoniacal. Apostles of this kind who become themselves objects of mortal worship are as the idols that carry in them the seed of God's vengeance. These counterfeiters cast out the true God from the hearts of men and place there their own false gods. God, who is the heart of every being, repelled by the manifestation of his absence, casts them into eternal confusion.

This exegesis is historical in a very profound sense; the history of souls is the texture of anecdotal history, its essential truth, the reason for its variations, as the microphysical is the reason for the physical: the swirling of waves does not result from reciprocal shocks, but from the laws of the depths in conjunction with the laws of the heavens. The historical exegesis which we permit in this parable requires anagogy, a transposition to a spiritual plane; and not only the parable, but the anecdotal history itself, require this new vantage point for a fuller understanding.

This is so necessary for our thesis that we take it upon ourself to stress what will serve as illustration to what we affirmed from the outset concerning the parable of the vine-dressers: a spiritual history which passes beyond mere time and space. It is not considered outside the realm of time for its light shines upon all ages; it does not stalk about in dream worlds or Platonic worlds of ideas: it is universal. The type of exegesis we adopt here does not permit us to curtail "the sacred history" condensed in the narrative of a usurped vineyard. The sacred history such as the Bible offers us is a remarkable application and significant image of the drama existing between Creator and free creature. Israel, the coming of Christ, the Church, constitute a totality which makes itself felt in many events; because the drama of creation

44

—and redemption—appears effectively there and is communicated there. The holy story is more than a sign revealing the underlying history; it has a certain sacramental value. But who stops at "the kinds and appearances" of the sacraments?

Let us be more precise. Israel is without doubt the chosen nation situated in Canaan where the Most High rules. It is the chosen vineyard, the hope of the future. But it is also the "remnant"[8] summing up and symbolizing the permanence of the servants of God in the world. Throughout the ages of paganism, others than Abraham kept their hearts faithful to God. Yesterday and today, there are souls polarized by the absolute, even if deviating myths hide from the true Israelites, that is to say, from the official believers, and from their own eyes, the truth of their quest of the divine. But the choice of Israel, of a people, does have the advantage of showing that fidelity is not strictly a personal affair. In spite of their ethnical and cultural distinctions, the faithful form—mystically—a real community.

However, if they have only the Law, only an ethical code or a cult, they are incapable of resisting the evil of the "property owner": the temptation to fill up the places reserved for God, to substitute for God. Whereas the pagans, ancient or modern, retain some distracted marking of the eternal One in their myths, and without being able to deceive the enlightened minds on the content of their theories, the Israelites of the Law, as we have seen, easily falsify the message of the Most High. The pagans divinize man and scarcely conceal it. The Pharisees proclaim the living God and kill his prophets, killing God in his prophets.

[8] Ez. 9, 8; 14, 22; Is. 49, 6.

They are the Grand Inquisitors. They pretend to control and exploit his divinity. The vineyard is for their use.

If there were but the four "major" and twelve "minor" prophets of God found in the Bible, it would imply only a sporadic and discontinuous activity on the part of him who is everywhere at work. Today as in ages past, the heralds of the Spirit are at grips with the Letter; charity is in conflict with legality, freedom with slavery. Thus it is that pulsing life rebels against the layer of crust choking it to death.

It is remarkable that the more devastating the abomination, the more numerous and magnificent the prophets are. Christ met face-to-face the abomination of the entire history of all men. He is not merely one of the prophets, the last one to rise up against it, the last and most important, just as the last member of a procession is the most important. He is that, but much more. He is the first and the only prophet, the Word of God. He is the type of everyone who speaks in the name of God, before him and after him in time. In them he prophesies, he suffers, he dies, gathering their deaths into his own sacrifice. Salvation is by no means anecdotal! Christ is the universal prophet of the Father's vineyard, and his ceaseless transcendent action is actualized in every age and place. If the Son dies, it is because the Law is unyielding to Charity. That explains the unchanging severity of the punishment.

Certainly, the fall, or rather the falls, of Jerusalem are found symbolically in each Testament. Since the time of man's sin, the destruction of Babels, the catastrophies of civilizations without God, or those set up against God, follow one right after the other. They are the external result of an internal break with the rhythm of created nature. Our own epoch stands in danger

46

of such an evil: and by the fact that these disasters related to the failure of the world include the innocent, even if they become redemptive victims, it is nonetheless evident that they can become expiators and that they do not correspond to the pitiless sanction which too much characterizes the Gospel of love, particularly evident in this parable: "What therefore will the owner of the vineyard do to them? He will come and destroy those vine-dressers." As the people protested against this, Christ fixed his gaze on them and declared: "What then is this that is written, 'The stone which the builders rejected, has become the cornerstone'? Everyone who falls upon that stone will be broken to pieces; but upon whomever it falls, it will grind him to powder."[9] The judgment is pitiless, it does not consider human weaknesses for which the Saviour is filled with tender mercy. He condemned evil: the hypocrisy, brimming with evil, doomed to nothingness. This condemnation flashes like lightning in the backdrop of the drama; it strikes only the people and civilizations as bolts of lightning strike the earth after a thunderstorm in the clouds. Creatures are struck only according to their secret and intimate collaboration with the powers that stir up creation. Temporal misfortune can from that time on be for the just a salvation through sacrifice, and for the indomitably evil, it is the prefiguration of the second death—the eternal death . . . —while for the others, it may be an occasion of salutary purification.

Moreover, after all this misfortune, "he will give the vineyard the city of evil. But the Church is the reassembly of the true to others."[10] The Church replaces Israel. Its temporal place faces

[9] Lk. 20, 15–18.
[10] Lk. 20, 16.

Israel, it is Abraham able to give his son to God in the total
sacrifice of the holocaust, and it is all the "saints" of paganism
whom we place under the thrilling patronage of the Church.
The Church is not Christ prolonged—it is Christ present. The
Mystical Body corresponds to his connection with humanity, at
least with those who accept the Law in its substance of charity
without draining its blood. Such is the universal, Catholic
Church, not yet all-embracing, but nevertheless all-inclusive by
right and essence, and at each moment, in every place in the
growth of humanity. All Christian actualities spring from the
Saviour's love and are bathed in its transcendence, in divine
Charity, not an ideal charity. This is what led Father Pouget to
say in speaking to Bergson of the overt religion: "We Christians
act in time, but we don't live in it." The visible society of the
Church, guided by the pastors' staffs, has the prophetical mission
to promote the Gospel and to communicate the Spirit of Pentecost to mankind on its journey down to the end of the world.
Like Christ, it can know agony and death in the last days. This
"spiritual supplement" which our modern civilization needs, has
the responsibility of communicating to it; it may not be successful
in spite of the allies it has everywhere among men of good will.
On the horizontal plane, it may be a defeat; but what matters is
that eventually it perpendicularly sets up the heavenly Jerusalem
immanent and transcendent over the earthly city.

The parable of the vine-dressers is, after all, optimistic. It invites us to raise ourselves up by virtue of the individual at first
(for adherence to freedom is the personal action of the individual), and by means of the social (for individuals by their acts
are joined to others and to the world), and as a result to the high

and real interior plateau where charity fights against the Law. "Jesus said to them, 'Amen, amen, I say to you, you seek me, not because you have seen signs, but because you have eaten of the loaves and have been filled. Do not labor for the food that perishes, but for that which endures unto life everlasting.' "[11] And that is what we have attempted in this commentary where we are not confined to the merely material kind of exegesis. "The spiritual battle," writes Rimbaud, "is just as fierce as the wars of men."[12] Our Saviour declares, "I have overcome the world."[13] It is finished. Victory has been won in the supreme sacrifice. When the Son was beaten to death, the vineyard which was saved was put into the hands of good vine-dressers.

For better or worse, the spiritual history of the individual and humanity is written by the hand of God in the depths of eternity: Mene, Tekel, Parsin.[14]

[11] Jn. 6, 26–27.
[12] *Une saison en enfer.*
[13] Jn. 16, 33.
[14] Dan. 5, 25–27.

The Workers at the Eleventh Hour

MATTHEW 20, 1–15

THE parable of the workers at the eleventh hour is clearly and intentionally disturbing, for in it we find injustice displayed with obvious cynicism. Right from the outset we are confronted with the evident will to turn everything upside down, to reverse established values. "Many who are first now will be last, and many who are last now will be first."[1] It is as though Christ has declared, "In heaven you will see what I mean! There will be an upheaval in the ranks; man's hierarchy will be utterly destroyed! God does not conform to ribbons, camails, or funeral ranks. You will behold the poor, dazed by their triumph, unchained from their cold attics or fetid rooming houses, enthroned forever above the rich and the mighty! Thus it will be: lampmakers ranked above kings and even presidents of nations; insignificant lay people above bishops or popes, and even certain repentant sinners above the foremost of the congregation."

[1] Mt. 19, 30.

A Curious Story

The Lord told the quaint story of the hiring. The Father is not one of those idle employers who leave for the Riviera or the Canary Islands while their overseers goad their workmen. He does not himself work in the vineyard. God does not make use of miracles permanently. He has entrusted his creation to men and he takes it upon himself to send his apostles who "will bear fruit," who will radiate his love and sow his thought. The comparison used here is the vineyard. The Father sends his vine-dressers there: "Go to work!"—"What's the pay?"—"One denarius! Agreed?"—"Agreed!" One denarius—that is, the wage for a day's work ... or the price of a life, if one supposes that evening represents death, the hour of retribution. The satisfied employer doles out what is due: this is the judgment—and he who says judgment—says justice. Would God dare violate justice?

Until evening approaches with its refreshing coolness, rest, and pay, the vineyard is a factory constantly demanding new workers, a vineyard stretching out as far as the eye can see, a vineyard as large as the world and whose work is not completed until the end of time, that final evening of humanity, the hour of the Last Judgment. It is a vineyard that needs spading, trimming, spraying—a vineyard which never grows in wisdom and health, but which always attracts fungi, plant-lice, and all kinds of scavenger birds. If wine rejoices the heart of man, it first causes that heart so much care that a single workman is not enough to relieve the anxiety, and neither are ten or a hundred ... the owner of the vineyard must go out time and again to look for others.

Consequently, the employer goes into the village to the market place where idle men marvel over the heroes of the sports arena. "Come, work for me!" He does not propose a denarius for their wage, but only a just salary. Ah! it will be indeed just! They trust him and go out to the vineyard, leaving the market place to the sun. Passing the other workers, they ask of them, "How much does he pay?"—"He told us one denarius." One denarius! And the workers newly arrived, and those coming in at the third, sixth, and ninth hours, figure out a wage-scale, for the master continues to call, returning again and again to the market place where men continually gather together to be idle or play. "I shall have," they figure, "three-quarters of a denarius—a half of one— a quarter."

They of the eleventh hour are convinced that they will draw little pay, but they intend to make the best of it: they do not deserve any more. But of course, if they had had gone to work sooner. . . . After all, why were they not called at daybreak? For, in this quite provocative parable, they were able to go into the vineyard. They were free men. They were "bored stiff" at home. As they had nothing to do, they ended up by going into the market place to occupy themselves with amusement. But they had nothing against work, the vineyard, or the employer—the proof: they went to work without arguing about it. But then, if the master is just towards all men, why were they not called sooner?

Obviously, he had his reasons. He is arbitrary, but being sparing in his words, he knows what he wants. He calls and does not explain. Why is that one baptized on the day of his birth, surrounded by Christians, and immediately launched into the Christian faith? Why is another only converted on the eve of his wedding, and another when he is advanced in years and has one foot in the grave, at the eleventh hour? Night approaches, dark with mystery, and the employer calls again. He relies on men whose lives have been nothing but pleasure and idleness. He seems to need them as much as the others who have been protected much earlier from idleness and vice. "Go to work! There is still some work left for you. It is good: the heat of noon has left us! You may join the others."

They accept his offer with a spirit of generosity, and they accept at once. The ones most hurt from unemployment and most wasted away with worldly diversions do not balk. Some will say, "A fine thing! They haven't worked for ages!" Yet if we really knew the price for being habitually out of work, we would not hesitate to admire the hiring of the workers at the eleventh hour, for doing nothing is much the same as doing evil. There we see a little light that is not to be placed under the bushel, and it is this light which helps us to understand the employer's conduct.

The day is at an end; the steward is settled behind his desk, his register lies open and his money bag untied. "Call them," the master demands, "and pay them their wages, beginning from the last even to the first." The men hired at the eleventh hour come up to the desk and are not very confident. One-twelfth of a denarius is not very much at all. They are sorry that they did not sweat under the hot sun all day long. And now the surprise! The steward counts out for them one denarius; they do not believe their eyes. He is unmoved; perhaps their eyes have deceived them? No, it is really true—a shining new denarius. They look up at the steward who is impassible and confident with what he has just done. Then they turn their eyes towards the master who rejoices in their joy. And they pocket their denarius with trembling hands. "Imagine that! My wife and children won't get over it!" Delighted, they forget to thank him, but their happiness is quite enough for the master.

At this point the "injustice" becomes apparent. Nothing is said until then, and even the employer—generous soul—plays a fine role. But in fact the "injustice" has already begun. It is not necessary to reproach the master for having chosen his workers for a little joy, for having unevenly divided the work to be done among them, for having shown an excessive generosity bordering on demagogy; there are limits to wisdom and there are also rules of mathematics to be respected here.

When the workers called at dawn saw the denarius shine in the hands of the last called, they became stupefied, and then smiles slowly formed across their lips as they began their very rational and equitable calculations: twelve denarii for those who have worked from daybreak on: a fortune!

But the steward, imperturbable, hands them one denarius, just one, no more but no less! "Master, there must be a mistake!" They wipe the glistening sweat off their foreheads. Their mental equilibrium is bowled over at this violation of the most elementary arithmetic. The steward is indifferent to their protesting. The master answers them categorically, "There is no error; in my administration there has never been a single mistake!"— "But . . ."—"But what?" The first-called are the most annoyed, they feel the most wronged: one denarius instead of twelve! "We will not have it, master, we will not put up with this!" They menacingly point out the last-arrived who already are fearful for their unhoped-for fortune: "They—they have only worked one small hour, and in the coolness of the day. We have carried the brunt of the day and heat. Our last hour was unbearable, being loaded down as it was with the toil of all the rest. And you have given them the same as us! This is unjust!" They do not hope for the twelve denarii now, but they nobly hope for the carrying out of justice. Their precise notion of what is right would be easily enough satisfied if the steward were to run after the favored ones who are beginning to slink away before this turn of events. "Wait! You there! Come back! There has been a mistake: you only have right to a twelfth of a denarius." The employer does not stir, and the steward merely yawns. The evil is consummated. The frustrated angry murmur of the workmen is lost in an empty silence. Still another property owner who knows nothing at all about social questions!

But after more than a minute of silence which seemed like eternity, the employer speaks. Calmly he addresses the workman who stirred up the most trouble. "My friend," he begins. And the men think: "Let him keep his 'my friend' for himself—that exploiter of the people. And to crown it all off he now pretends to be just!" "I have done you no wrong whatever. Did we not agree for a denarius? Take what is yours and go. . . ." Of course, it would be just, if the others had not been there. Would that he had left them to their idleness and sports arenas! Legally he is right . . . but morally!

"I wish," the master continues, "to give to the last even as to you. Have I not a right to do what I choose?" The man, all confused, steps back. He is beaten. The master is master; he does not have to give any explanation; who would dare teach him a lesson and judge his liberalities? He might even take away the denarius which he has earned and which is the cause of the whole quarrel—for he dared to question the master, and the others followed suit. Does man have any rights before God? Here we guess the tone of voice in which Yahweh replied to a complaining Job—and it is the voice of a hurricane.

His voice rumbles like thunder: "Are you envious because I am generous?" Jealous and without love the first-called feel driven to the very brink of hell just because they wanted to defend their own kind of justice, but it is a fact that what one can defend with the most confidence is not always what one feels most. Our problems are always the best studied. Yet these workers come-in at daybreak seem to be condemned here, or at least threatened with damnation because they were treated as the least of the least. Certainly, this is not being "just." Now we get the impression they will only be saved by a goodness which forgives, a kind of well-meaning "injustice" on the part of the master. The master was unjust towards them, but they were unjust right to his face because they saw him as "unjust" and did not understand that he was good. But they are the ones who, indirectly, were not just to the last-hired of the workers regardless of how scandalously they were favored, because it is a strange and terrible injustice which does not distinguish between the one who suffers and the one who loves. If someone does not understand, it is because he does not love. The first obligation is to love; every heart expects love, and furthermore, one's neighbor has a just right to this love. If one is not loved, the unfolding of

56

his personality and his joy are jeopardized; he is injured and the order of creation is disrupted.

Exegesis in the Light of Love

"I am generous!", God declares with bitterness. And yet he categorizes the just with the wicked. Yes, this he does, for they are falsely just. The key to this parable—that golden key to the understanding of the divine mystery—is love. The moralist clad in the armor of justice, the judge of others, does not know love. The egalitarian who reduces all things to his own advantage, to his point of view, is incapable of rising up to the understanding of the Word of God. He is envious. He who loves, who sees the universe with an unclouded eye as God sees it, a world where all is joy in the heart of the man when he knows other hearts are rejoicing, a world where all is in mourning when the skitterish lamb is caught up in the brambles: the ninety-nine just do not weigh heavily in the heart which loves the impetuous one that only acts recklessly. Put on, then, the optic of love and not the optic of mathematics to judge God's justice and his "fantasies" towards the first and last workers of the vineyard.

The vineyard is the spiritual Church where man's mission is to work together with his fellow man for the day when the wine will stream into the wine vats and intoxicate all those who thirst for justice—the justice of the Bible which has nothing to do with social claims, but which is grace and virtue, a harmonizing of the soul to God, a holiness, not a quantum of wisdom acquired in the Law, but something living which makes the soul the joy of God. The mystical wine of charity is the drink of the just and they are just who labor for the well being of men in order that all men may drink and recognize in their enthusiasm that the Lord is good!

God, Personal Gift

The denarius signifies heaven, the reward for a good Christian life, not an entrance fee to gain access to the Beatitude, to the flower gardens, or to the chicken house accordingly as one either is first or last. It is life suddenly fulfilled, the outcome of existence hidden until then which shines in eternal peace. And how is this victory of the good workman possible, except by an encountering of his love with the absolute love? The denarius, earned throughout every minute as though the steward did not cease giving it, is the heaven of our soul, the manifestation of an infinite love which is only revealed at the moment of death. That is the marvelous prospective offered to men: being pulled out of the quicksand they will be able to receive from God this incomparable gift which is not split up: God himself!

God is the denarius which, whether first or last, the workers of the human community may obtain if they hold their hands wide open. If in heaven there are differences among the chosen ones, then it does not come from this Gift God has made of himself, but from the offering of our love, for just like a flower, the soul is opened up according to its measure, either more or less, to the Sun that shines for all with the same brilliancy. But there we must add that these are not quantitative differences, but rather a person-to-person relationship.

Reward for a Choice

Everyone who has worked in the vineyard has answered the call of love. The hour matters little. God does not consider the duration of the work, but the interior sentiment that germinates in the workmen, animating them. Now in the parable, Christ emphasizes that all have responded, as the master had hoped. Apparently, they are equal; they all knew how to answer with submission and zeal, "I am here." The responsibility for the delay of the last man falls to the lot of the employer—each soul has its hour foreseen from all eternity. We saw at Cana that Jesus' hour—that miraculous hour of God—had come. If all men were converted in the same hour, would there still be need for apostles; if all men were immediately good, how could we exercise patience? Evil has a definite role in the evolution of the universe as a dog rolling a barrel in which it has been enclosed. Whatever be God's design for souls, the important thing is to be there when he passes by, even though we be the least of sinners. The important thing is to say "yes." It is necessary and sufficient to be a soul of good will. The apostles have left everything else to follow after him. The young rich man would have been an apostle, had he renounced his ephemeral goods, even after the call of the twelve. St. Paul, in order to have been called the last, the one born out of due time,[2] did not become the least with St. Peter, the first of all the apostles. He was struck with a blinding light. He was not refused on the road to Damascus. Yet, he did not waste away his time in the market place, and instead he ran into the vineyard to ravage it.

[2] 1 Cor. 15, 8.

We would not be surprised to learn that the worker at the eleventh hour complained because he was called too late; as St. Augustine lamented: "Lord, late have I loved you!" We hear him raise up his voice in sorrow to the Lord and these are his words: "If you would have called me at daybreak, I would have worked with all my heart for you; should I have to work the whole night through, I would be ready." Yes, the Good Thief would willingly come down from the cross to serve such a generous Lord.

True Judgment

We cannot judge God in our ignorance, nor can we judge our neighbor: we shall, in fact, be judged by our love. The good are they who correspond with total generosity at the moment of grace which is love. But who will say, who will know, the intention of each one? Is he who protests against last-minute conversions truly a worker in the vineyard, a man in God's service for the good of men? Does he not deserve the title "envious"? He wants to form God to the cut of his own jealousy. He wants a God "for himself." His is an attitude we shall meet again in the elder brother of the prodigal son. The reaction of the workmen of the first hour is the sign of an egotistical mentality which they did not break away from during their work. The way they treated the master reveals them to themselves and to others. How many are called to the faith from infancy and live as formalistic Christians! How many pull themselves together little by little after having been given the strength! Blessed are they who pray for eleventh-hour conversions and who rejoice with the heart of little Thérèse when the criminals kissed the crucifix and gained heaven at that last blessed hour when the justice of men howled for their necks!

The Talents

MATTHEW 25, 14–30

TRANSPOSING the word "talent" from the mercantile economy to the spiritual economy is not especially difficult, since today we no longer use it to mean a monetary unit, but use it rather to signify natural gifts, particularly those of intelligence, imagination, and will. . . . By it we also mean manual skill and comeliness which are assets one does not earn but which must be utilized properly.

If, in other respects, we say that someone has a talent, we do not only mean real gifts, but also the end result of a gift which has been developed. The talent acquired by a divine force at work in the individual is usually the more admired; in fact, that admiration transcends the one possessed from above and turns to adore God. The talent remains on the more human level; it is from heaven, but in the hands of man. It is closely linked to a man's actions.

Divine Gifts

Let us be quite clear about the necessary transposition to the spiritual plane: it is a question of grace, that divine life communicated to each man, and it is also a question of what we call graces, that procession of favors descending to us from our heavenly Father. We are also fundamentally concerned with natural grace, the gift of existence and of all that qualifies our existence, where the supernatural comes into play, flowing in and branching out in such a way that life and action may only be considered as dependent on salvation, dependent on the deification reserved for the adopted sons of God.

The talents signify man such as he is. St. Paul wrote, "But by the grace of God I am what I am."[1] St. Augustine tells us, "Become what you already are!" God has a notion of each of us, which we call "ideal," to which a vocation, a mission, corresponds, and we must actualize it. "Become what you already are in the thought . . . in the hope of God!" This divine idea is set in motion within our being from its first dawning into the world by creation and redemption; it is in us as a potential something exerting pressure and which tends to be actualized, but which will only be fully materialized when our freedom is not opposed to it and collaborates in the realization in us of the eternal plan.

Let us leave the scholars to discuss among themselves the monetary value of the gold talent of 42kg 533! Let us try better to understand the spiritual lesson of this parable. "For it is like a man going abroad, who called his servants and handed over his

[1] 1 Cor. 15, 10.

63

goods to them."[2] By his infinite transcendence God is absent from his creation, but he remains present to it, not to say immanent, by the goods, his goods, which he accords it so that on the glorious day of his return the servant will be his son. "His" goods: therefore, it is a question of what is divine or related to the divine in man. The servant, having been called, summoned, receives a marvelous trust—God's own possessions which, by an unbelievable extension, are also the created riches of God, and not only the uncreated, not only God himself, but his entire creation—everything which is evident to the breath of the Spirit! The expression "servant" indeed signifies that man, by nature, is a subject being, but more so that he has received the duty, the mission to continue creation, the work of God, as much in these works as in his own existence.

God is, in fact, always present, always acting, but according to his divine plan; and we have the feeling of working here alone, while the filigree of his divine power winds through our lives and all our actions. Everything depends on God, and we have to act as though everything depended on us alone, but according to the order which manifests the freedom of the Creator. Creatures are not created equal; the capacity for the divine is different between the material and spiritual, as it is among men where it varies from soul to soul. The characteristic of the divine gift is that grace perfectly suits the individual's nature; water perfectly fills up the river bed at its source; the sun perfectly fills up a crystal or a diamond with itself. Justice is no more equal than river beds or precious stones . . . and everything is created to be filled; happiness must embody precisely the receptive appetite of

[2] Mt. 25, 14.

64

each being, and then it is a question of our action being free, the overture of our freedom.

Collaborators with God

"And to one he gave five talents, to another two, and to another one, to each according to his particular ability, and then he went on his journey." Three categories which actually sum up the whole varied range, beginning first with men called to holiness, then to those who are called to be exemplary Christians, and finally ending with those who have been called to be the soldiers of the Church. It is certain that He who calls at any hour, calls servants of every qualification, complementing each other, forming by their coordination and concatenation the perfection of the People of God. Little Thérèse of the Child Jesus was chosen from before her birth. Themes of inherited sanctity ran through her fiber; the lessons, the examples she received trained her internal music to be used and to sing out in her life. Her joys and hardships were orchestrated for a wonderful symphony. She had the freedom to engulf this splendor in cacophony—everything was given her to fulfill a destiny which God, we daresay, needed for other Christians and for all men.

The soldiers of the Church and humanity have not received so great a talent. They are sometimes born with an unfortunate inheritance; immorality rages round about them. Yet they have received something, if only a fantastic capacity to endure. Amid the refuse of centuries of sin, the least of souls have still got a flower from heaven. This disproportion seems unjust, cruelly unjust. But we know it is true, whether we like it that way or not. We desire simply to understand! Why this injustice? Why does God not heed the Declaration of the Rights of Man?

The one who received much immediately began to develop his talents; he is zealous. He does not say he is already rich, that he has something to do, that God has ordered nothing from him, or expressly commanded him to do something; he does not take it into his head to profit by laziness and egotism, by living off his rents from the Being of God, the Grace of God. He uses these gifts according to their nature; they have been given him to increase. These talents are not gold, and yet economists manage to make gold multiply itself—the gold lives, in a sense, and increases in the bankers' hands. God's talents are participations in his Being, his Life, and his Love. They are a sharing in God's commitment to the world, a participation in his action which is creation and redemption. He who is clothed with this divine dynamism, must be, according to St. Paul's way of asking it, a worker together with God.[3] The servant with five talents sets to work at once, both in himself and in his milieu to accomplish what God began, to perfect what is lacking in every created being. In the same fashion, with his teacher's instruction, the student must complete the page on which the first letters have been traced.

The Dynamism of Divine Gifts

We do not put the lamp under a bushel;[4] we do not seal ourselves off from the light like canned sardines. We do not prevent the seed from growing, the tree from blossoming and bursting

[3] 2 Cor. 6, 1.
[4] Mt. 5, 15–16.

out in fruit, without drying up the source and killing the tree. *"Bonum est diffusum sui!"* "Goodness is diffused of itself." He who has the goods of God has light and life in him. They must be shared. They possess their rhythm, their law: love. And no one holds them in deposit as treasures in a storehouse.

The first two servants follow this law of charity. They do not create goods—what man is capable of doing that? They act in such a way that God's goods fulfill all their secret potentialities. We possess nothing we have not received and we can do nothing which is not in potency in what is given us. That is why all the gifts of God are from the "love due."[5] Opposite God, justice is not equalitarian: it does not suppress and it is not a waster of the given potential. From the parable of the foolish and wise virgins we learn that it is of utmost importance to have enough oil. He who does not have the desired surplus, and who lacks generosity and does just what has simply got to be done, is condemned. Pascal well understood this when he revolted against casuistry; he did not understand that casuistry is a science of justice, but not the law of those of us—all men—who have to be judged. If our law is to figure out how far we can go before falling into mortal sin, if our soul's intention is to skim the abyss of hell and to live religion to the minimum, to do just what is absolutely necessary to still "be in" the state of grace, it is certain then that our spiritual condition is worse than the sinner's who is swept away by the tide of his passions, against even the evangelical spirit.

However, it is this spirit which animates the servant who has

[5] An expression of Richard of St. Victor to connote the response between love received and love given.

received but the one talent. "But he who had received the one went away and dug in the earth and hid his master's money."[6] The act of digging is one closely related to death; by digging and burying he performs an action associated with death! It is a work of darkness: he is hiding! Because of jealousy? Hardly! He buries the talent because of justice, because of legalistic, literal, and formalistic justice; he is a servant of the Letter which kills. Moreover, he clearly explains himself with a note of antipathy in his voice, when at the master's return he is reproached for not having done as the others. Oh, he didn't want to run risks; adventure displeases him; he is a prudent man. He received one talent and he will give one back. The master cannot criticize this act for he will not have been robbed of anything! And yet he will have been robbed of much love, robbed of the surplus his goods normally produce. The servant will not have been a good servant, because he will not have acted for his master and because he will not have reciprocated the master's kindness with his own kindness—the master's goods with his goods. When we truly love, we do more, always more, not for ourselves, but for the satisfaction, the well being of the beloved. A servant without love is found wanting in the spiritual kingdom whose law is love. He would have chanced love and lost—but can one lose in a domain where the intention counts eminently?—, he would have been forgiven. Doubtless, he does not understand Péguy when he places both the sinner and the saint in the same category.

The servant of the Law, incapable of returning a "gift" for a gift, finds the exactingness of love not only unjustified, and

[6] Mt. 25, 18.

thereby unjust, but also cruel. "Master, I know that you are a stern man; you reap where you have not sowed and you gather where you have not winnowed; and because I was afraid, I went away and hid your talent in the earth; behold, you have what is yours." The unfortunate man—he condemned himself. He did not accept the gift from heaven which makes up his whole life as a child of God, he did not make it his own; he did not stop to think that if God would take back what he has given, only his nothingness would remain. That he was afraid is normal. Love is always frightening to the worldly-wise; it causes a thousand follies, privations, sacrifices, martyrdoms, in short it forms the follies of the saints into the image of Christ's folly. The priest in *The Power and the Glory*[7] says to the atheist lieutenant, "We wouldn't recognize *that* love. It might even look like hate. It would be enough to scare us—God's love. It set fire to a bush in the desert, didn't it, and smashed open graves and set the dead walking in the dark?" This fear drove the young rich man away from Jesus, though he nonetheless scrupulously practiced the Law.[8] How they fear the daily routine of perfection and the burning Spirit who, in the night of the senses, and thought as well, transfigures the man, leads him into the Holy Trinity, and fills him with bliss. The "good and faithful" servants, faithful to the Law of Goodness, enter into the joy of their Lord. How many are frightened off by this superhuman joy which is not theirs, which is only gained by renouncing worldly goods and

[7] A novel by Graham Greene. See Part III, Chapter III, p. 269, of the Viking Press Compass Books edition.
[8] Mt. 19, 16–22.

at the expense of countless battles! How many are frightened off by this joy which is the superhuman gift of God to those cast into the furnace of his love as burnt offerings!

The master who calls the unproductive servant "wicked and slothful," does not contradict him at heart: "You knew that I reap where I do not sow, and gather where I have not winnowed? You should therefore have entrusted my money to the bankers, and on my return I should have got back my own with interest."[9] This stern text is magnificent with liberality on the spiritual level. God is not interested in the putting up of money —he is not interested in the five, the two, or the one talent. He wanted the lily, the rose, the violet, and the dandelion. He loves the last as much as the others; in any event, he will never reproach it for being what it is; because it is required for the success of universal harmony. Upon returning from his voyage, God wishes to give, not what is his, his money, but properly his servants' gain, that which is their own and that which they give to him, the fruit of their efforts, the testimony of their good will. Men are created free agents and are therefore capable of responding to love; they have a debt of love, five or two or one talent; but they have to do better; they can also, like God, love and give. Without a doubt, the matter of their gifts comes from the munificence of God: they take their start from him, the dynamic potential and the permanent fulcrum which permit the man to dare surpass himself, to aspire to living according to God, by the very Law of God which is Charity. Every man can and must give of himself to live the spirit of love which is free, outside the realm of all accountability, not even that of the harvest or the garnering.

[9] Mt. 25, 26–27.

A man's grandeur is precisely the dignity which God conferred on him and which permits him to give to God. That is what makes man to be the image of God, living the same law, the law of more than fifty-fifty—the law of charity. The faithful servants, therefore, are the true sons of God; they have the same spirit! They were created to live together, together in the same happiness.

Just Punishment

We shall note that he who does not know how to rise up to generosity is he who has received the least. The justice of God's love expects a proportional response, very much more demanding of the most favored than of the least favored. The widow's mite enkindles more admiration than the liberal offerings of the rich, because she gave all she had.[10] Had the rich man given all his possessions, he would have been comparably admired. Very much more is required of the one to whom much has been given, and little is required from the others, and the intention counts more than the "matter" of the act. Thus the servant who did not clearly understand God's will, who did things deserving of stripes, "will be beaten with few stripes."[11]

If in the parable the least favored servant is the unfaithful one, it does not mean that he—this half-paid one—is practically damned and that the mass of idle servants, dedicated as the foolish virgins to exterior darkness, are recruited from among people like him. Christ meant the favored have received what is

[10] Lk. 21, 1–4.
[11] Lk. 12, 48.

71

sufficient for them: they have only to draw upon themselves to realize their spiritual duty. The advice to those who only have the one talent is to give it over to bankers whose business it is to increase the goods entrusted to them. Who are they who help us love, who guide us onto the path of sacrifice, of virtue, and bestowal, if not the Christian who feels responsible for his fellow man, who takes the apostolate to heart, who has the mission to direct his neighbor to the path of perfection? May he who feels himself incapable, but who is desirous of advancing in love, humbly call upon those whose vocation it is to assist the poor!

One would think we have exhausted this parable's teaching. But that is not the case! Something still rubs against our egalitarian grain. The master, in condemning him who didn't know how to love, declares: "Take away therefore the talent from him, and give it to him who earned ten talents over and above the ten given him. For to everyone who has shall be given, and he shall have abundance; but from him who does not have, even that which he seems to have shall be taken away."[12] We have already said that the useless servant condemned himself for not having anything: "Behold, you have what is yours!"[13] He wants nothing from God, especially not the power of love God gives. Therefore, it is nothing surprising that the talent was taken away from him, but is it not outside the realm of all justice that it was given to the one who increased his ten? Is it not a singularly disturbing thing, and is it not small of him when seen in the light of its cruelty? So it seems on the material plane.

[12] Mt. 25, 28–29; see Mk. 4, 24–25.
[13] Mt. 25, 25.

And Exacting Reward

What recompense does the master give his faithful servants? "Because you have been faithful over a few things, I will set you over many. . . ."[14] In the analogous parable of the gold pieces, the master gives his most faithful servant authority over ten towns in his kingdom.[15] The talents which seem a fabulous treasure are nothing compared to the new treasure which will be entrusted to the zealous servant. A difficult mission is reserved for him by way of showing appreciation—a mission in which he will find happiness, for this man likes to serve. He is the man in the lord's trust. ". . . and of him to whom they have entrusted much, they will demand the more."[16] As a reward, the faithful servant is given charge over all his goods.[17]

Clearly, it is not a question of entrusting anything whatever to one who does not already understand, and particularly one who had no desire to dedicate himself. One gives only to the rich. This fact is as true on the spiritual plane as on the temporal—but what a truth it is! They are always the same ones who volunteer to work when there is need of dedication, of unassuming work to be done, when there is need of generosity freed of pride, we always have recourse to the same ones—who are already overburdened and who never say "no." It is strange that those who have nothing important to do, always think they are bullied,

14 Mt. 25, 21–23.
15 Lk. 19, 11–27.
16 Lk. 12, 48.
17 Lk. 12, 44.

victims of fate, and exploited. They do not stop their working—
those who scarcely have time to breathe, who have not got one
moment "to themselves," who have given their all and are still
able to undertake new obligations and do them well. Every man
who has some degree of love possesses a force which seems infinitely extendable, because it draws its source in the infinite. He
can always take on an extra task: love immediately waxes strong
in him so that he is equal to his new mission. We are then
beyond the realm of calculation. We are dealing with a man
whose zeal is devouring him; if he dies at his tasks it is because
his mission is accomplished: his sacrifice is consummated; he
dies, joyful in the work he has performed, and he rejoices in his
master's joy.

Can the master abandon a single part of creation entrusted to
the care of men? If there are quitters, deserters, or simply lazy
men in the frontlines of redemption, it is quite necessary that the
good soldiers take their place and sacrifice themselves for them.
The saints carry the sinners on their shoulders and the weight
of the world does not crush them. They have the strength of love
in them, the strength of God.

It is a strange parable in which the laws of justice and initial
preferences in a judgment favoring one who already has abundance of goods are so often scoffed at. However, it well supple-
ments the parable of the ten virgins and the workers in the
vineyard. This one throws light, a very realistic light, on the
divine economy; it teaches one who would be discouraged by
his feeble spiritual capacity, that he already has much—one talent
is quite a fortune!—and it teaches that this divine good is an
immense possibility, if he but know how to be a collaborator

with God. Nor is he discouraged by jealousy because others have more eminent vocations. What God sees is not the gift he has advanced to each, with so much diversity, but rather he sees the gifts which each uses to correspond to his goodness, his desires, and the requirements of his love. He who has received more, has graver responsibilities; he will be judged accordingly. But in a word, the joy of God is offered to all who respond to him with good will to the utmost capacity of their heart!

The Wise and Foolish Virgins

MATTHEW 25, 1–13

THEY knocked on the door. They began pounding on it, and anxiety took hold of them. It was not possible, he would not leave them outside of the wedding feast; he had not heard their knock. They pounded harder: "Lord, Lord, open for us!" The pitiless answer came to them, "I know you not."[1] It was as though they did not exist for him. They felt themselves sliding off into nothingness.

Divine Injustice?

The foolish virgins considered themselves little guilty. Surely they had been negligent, and they even admitted it, but their conduct was not so different from that of the prudent virgins as to deserve this implacable rejection. The groom showed himself without love and justice for their behalf. We can readily see he was without love. But was he unjust?

The wise virgins carried their lamps, their lighted lamps, their

[1] Mt. 25, 12.

lamps filled with oil and throwing off light. They went out with
their oil to meet the bridegroom . . . and as he was late, they
grew sleepy close by the other virgins, and they fell asleep as did
the others. It was night and they stopped watching for his arrival
and stopped talking. They fell into a very deep sleep. Not one
of them stood watch—and the bridegroom did not reproach either
the prudent or the foolish for having closed their eyes. They kept
their ears open while sleeping. They all heard the cry in the
night: "Behold, the bridegroom is coming, so go forth to meet
him!"[2] They awoke together and hurried to prepare their lamps:
they all did, the foolish as well as the wise. The foolish virgins
were not merely foolish! If they were only foolish, they would
have been irresponsible but the door to the wedding feast would
not have been closed to them. They were imprudent: they took
their trimmed lamps, but they had no extra oil with them. They
had not foreseen that the bridegroom might be late in coming.
Now he was late and their lamps were almost burned dry.

If the foolish erred it was here . . . in trying to redress their
error. They appealed to the wise virgins, to the "smart" virgins,
as we say. They were no more sympathetic than the unfaithful
servant would have been had we been compelled to keep to the
level of the story such as is told. No, they gave nothing, not even
one single drop of oil. They answered like perfect egotists, "Lest
there may not be enough for us and for you, go rather to those
who sell it, and buy some for yourselves."[3] The five silly women
then ran to the oil merchants to buy some oil, and while they
were gone the bridegroom came and it was then they erred. They

[2] Mt. 25, 6.
[3] Mt. 25, 9.

were not there to meet him. We may ask ourselves whether it would not have been better for them had they waited humbly, filled with confusion and sorry, for him who is the Prince of Forgiveness. In fact, they were no less virgin than the others, they were just as attentive as the others, they did not sleep any more than the others, but they were gone when the bridegroom came because listening to the cruel advice of their friends, they went out at midnight to pound on the door of the oil merchant.

Is it really necessary to know why the virgins had no torches, but only tiny lamps, and is it necessary to discover whether they kept watch for him along the roadside or at the house of the betrothed, etc.? The problem—or the mystery—is the fact that the foolish women found themselves excluded from the kingdom of heaven at the last moment, in spite of their good intentions, because of a negligence void of any true malice. How can we not experience unrest at an interpretation of this kind which at least has merit in not being like some others which exalt watchfulness or vigilance? Misfortune befalls the one who does not keep watch! The wise kept watch; their lamps watched. We know that the foolish virgins were no worse.

The Fault of the Foolish Virgins

We have to transpose to the spiritual level. It is obvious the bridegroom is God or Christ. He is going to come. . . . When he has gathered his faithful together, then his kingdom will come, that place of love symbolized in the wedding feast: an ecstasy of infinite joy shared by all the members of the Mystical Body. Heaven is shown in all respects as a communal *agapē,* more than a fraternal one, or nuptial feast. The communion of the mystical marriage is heaven. Where is the bride? She seems unimportant in this parable. Some have suggested that she is the Church or the Virgin Mary. It is our own belief that the omission was intentional: the ten virgins are given such importance because they represent the souls who are all called to the heavenly wedding feast. We may imagine that behind these virgins is summed up the towering presence of the Church, the spouse of Christ, which only has existence in her members.

We are speaking here of the faithful, the practicing faithful, who have their moments of human weakness, who occasionally fall asleep, but not with the sleep of mortal sin: they are able to rise up at once and they do what they must so as not to stall the wedding feast, their feast, their wedding. Again we are not speaking of great sinners or those fervent with heroic virtues. The virgins, wise or foolish, are apparently and confusedly the ragged soldiery of Christians. But something of capital importance separates them, condemning some and saving others. The principle of a radical distinction between souls is a subtle thing, little evident to our understanding, and it is this principle which is characteristic of this parable as with the others, and with life. Ours is the mentality of the Pharisees and doctors of the Law: either we do not perceive this distinction or we give it little value.

The important distinction to be made is that the foolish virgins did not take any flasks of oil with them so they might have an extra supply of oil. Why, then, does this negligence present such grave consequences?

We usually say that the light of their lamps is the faith which is diffused. But the oil which anoints and illumines is the image of the Holy Spirit who diffuses charity into souls, who makes them children of God, "capable of God," according to St. Bernard. They are the virgins capable of merit, capable of entering into that eternal feast with the Bridegroom. Everything is given them in abundance and superabundance for that one purpose. The love which is given has no limits; it is something coming from infinite reserves to satisfy.

What is the difference between the foolish and the wise? It is this: The foolish are made foolish by too much human wisdom. When the wise do not calculate and act according to the direction of their hearts, they are overwhelmed with the foolish wisdom of charity. But the foolish, they too take only what is absolutely necessary in their little egotistical opinion; just what they have got to take. They want no more of love than is necessary to their ungenerous hearts. The wise did not take extraordinary amounts of oil, fabulous sums of charity! No, they took only a little more, acting outside the realm of reason, as is normal for those in love to do. Their love is understood in that *little more* which shows their spirit of sacrifice—the spirit of the Bridegroom. The foolish—who thought themselves wise, being daughters of the Law more than of Charity—had their little idea of God, of a God made in the measure of man, a plaything of man. They act as though God were not transcendent and on quite another level, where reason counts as nothing. They act as if God were not perplexing, for God is always on time, he always arrives on time, but at *his* time! They who open their souls as much as possible to the Holy Spirit, without understanding God any more than the others, and although they behave to excess, they are in fact the wise. Their excess filled up God's tardiness, filled up the indifference between God's hour and man's, transcended the gulf between Creator and creature. A few drops of oil, a few drops of true charity are sufficient to raise up the bark of the wise virgins to the height of God. . . .

Of course, they were not perfect. In their blatantly obvious negligence they seemed no better than the rest. But when they awoke, they still had their "more than sufficient" oil, the oil of *gratuitous love.*[4] The foolish who fashioned God into a creature more to their liking, who supposed that justice was enough, who thought it sufficient to give like for like, who had only required love in their hearts, who contented themselves with just the foreseeable obligation prescribed and imposed by the Law, who followed the code and fulfilled the required minimum, but who did not know how to respond to the impulse of a generous heart, they awoke with the other virgins, but the bridegroom had already passed them by. These virgins, formalistic, narrow-minded, and limited in spirit, closed in on themselves by their way of human measurement, and locking in their God with them, awoke with the others to meet the bridegroom, but God had already passed them by. They loved with a love called concupiscence,[5] and not with a love of sacrifice, and it was as though they had not loved at all. They were not passed by; they always wanted to possess God, the happiness of God, and they had always wanted to take their places in the feast. Now, God is not possessed; he gives himself to those who give themselves. Since he

[4] Gratuitous or free love. This is the expression dear to Richard of St. Victor. This is a disinterested love, the gift of one's self.

[5] As opposed to a gratuitous love, corresponding to desire, to mercenary love, but not to the love of the flesh.

gives everyone the power to give himself, the foolish virgins were culpable; they refused these secret graces, these entreaties, these invitations to cut themselves off from the mercenary, commercial faith, for a life entirely given to God without selfish motives. Usually these inclinations spring from trifling things, slight temptations, or arise in the face of human distress. We do not know when or how the foolish virgins came to be that way from too much human wisdom and their confining religion, but we do know that when they awoke their lamps had gone out.

They announced, they cried out the bridegroom's imminent arrival. Death—God's herald—was there, and they noticed suddenly that even their justice had shriveled up to nothing. The mistakes of an indifferent life, and all the negligences and inactivities of it, are sufficient to exhaust every bit of justice and right of that individual before the face of God. Even a task correctly performed—and who can claim such a thing?—does not count. The generosity of a selfless heart alone matters—that and all the sacrifices accomplished in this state of unselfishness. Everything a man gives or loses here below, he gains back, earned for eternity. Charity alone gives the right (if we may say this) to enter into heaven into the mystical marriage, for it alone corresponds to divine Charity. Now, the bride—and all the bride's friends—must become like the bridegroom. Love demands this harmony for the sake of union.

Incommunicable Charity

Because of their indifferent lives, the wise virgins squandered their strict rights to eternity, but their charity remains. The foolish virgins, having only the night in which to warm their souls to God, took fright. They were going to lose "their" heaven. "Give us some of your oil," they begged.[6] Now, they asked for precisely what their companions, in spite of their charity, were unable to share. God may give us the grace to love, the freedom capable of loving, the grace which is the new strength of freedom, but he himself cannot love for us, and that is the reason for hell. God cannot force a man to love. . . . The wise virgins had the greatest reason in the world for being powerless to help their sisters. Salvation, like love, is a strictly individual, personal, and incommunicable affair. Generosity was why these souls did not count before God, just as stifling egotism was for the foolish virgins. Sometimes one can pay another's debts, but if he has contracted debts, then one cannot give out money for them. The wise virgins were unable to rewrite the past by changing the foolish women's egotism into charity, or past egotism into past charity, which was inscribed forever in the history of each one.

But we may always help a soul choose God and wake up to true love through our example, by our advices and all the different means which set up a favorable environment around these souls so that they may arise to the dawning of the virtue of sacrifice. The wise virgins, unable to love God less, who, even for their neighbor, could not possibly consent to diminish their charity, advised their unfortunate companions to run to the merchants: "Go rather to those who sell it, and buy some for yourselves." Loving is perhaps the only thing one cannot do for others. "Try to love! Try to love as we love!" was the wise virgins' counsel, and in reality it was not ironical, hard, or pitiless.

[6] Mt. 25, 8.

83

They could do nothing else. We must die for our neighbor, but we cannot lose our soul for him.

What can simple and generous Christian souls advise—they who are not themselves lost in the mystical heights—what can they recommend to bewildered souls at the threshold of eternity, except to go find a priest, the intermediary and dispenser of grace? They who advise turning to the Holy Spirit actually give the same advice, for priests only dispense the gifts of God if the request is according to the Holy Spirit. There is necessarily a commerce, an admirable commerce, as the liturgy of the incarnation says. There is a very ancient tradition which tells us that Christ should have declared, "The kingdom of heaven is like unto a commerce." But what is less mercantile than the Gospel? This business transaction is an exchange of love, a dialogue of love which is not realized on a level of equality and justice, but between a transcendent Being and limited, created being, a slave risen up to sonship with God.

The wise virgins advise, "Go and buy from the sellers of oil," but to obtain the oil of charity we need a spirit of love. A soul praying to the Holy Spirit asks, "I want to love my God, give me to Him," and he will not be refused. It is written: "Ask and you shall receive. Seek and you shall find." Because of this promise people burn candles in churches so that they might win a good position, a satisfactory income, or the person one is in love with—this I know! Yet if we are patient enough to read the sacred text without rushing through it, we learn we are dealing with the Spirit of holiness, goodness, the Spirit of love.[7] It is the only value, the only gift, which God will never refuse. If we ask

[7] Mt. 7, 7–12; Mk. 11, 24–25; Lk. 11, 9–14; Jn. 14, 13–17.

God for happiness, either here below or in heaven, we pretend to put God to our use, to make him yield to our desires however petty or great they may be. And we become gluttons ready to swallow up the Creator as well as the whole of creation. It is the triumph of egocentrism to lay hands on God, to "have" him to use. The gift of love alone puts man into the proper perspective with God—who is beyond all measure and alone the center of everything which is. A force sustained by grace alone gives man his true meaning. Egotism, running after its nothingness, desirous of hoarding all things in its nothingness, completely lacks the right orientation and just direction which is the infinite depth wherein he who loses all refinds all things in the ecstatic goodness of God. Were our "senseless" virgins, running to the oil merchants, disposed to change the "direction" of their lives? Did they want to become wise again?

I Do Not Know You

In the night of their souls, they, obsessed with themselves, pounded on the door of the oil merchants. What is the significance of the bridegroom? He is the entrance way into the banquet hall which must not fail. Now, they lacked the necessary admittance fee because they lacked the least receptivity to charity. Had the priests been able to give them all the oil flasks in the world, all the sacraments, the oil of grace would have rolled right off the back of each of them. Their lamps could not be relighted. The foolish virgins decided to go up to the door of the wedding feast which shut them off from the bridegroom and wise virgins. From then on this parable makes no more mention of their lamps. They cried out: "Lord, Lord, open to us!" They did not say: "We are wrong! We did not know how to go out of ourselves, how to forget ourselves in order to love! Forgive us for not having responded to your love! Grant us the folly of loving, of loving you, which no one has yet been able to teach us!" Such a prayer would have been answered. The bridegroom himself might have gone out, shouting with joy. He himself would have brought the oil: "Enter into my heart! I lost you and here you are living, here at last you are beginning to love, at last you think no more of your own good fortune! Finally you are filled with the desire of giving yourselves! My joy is exalted a hundredfold. Enter! You do not seek your own petty happiness, but you seek mine instead. Love, not happiness, must be the final end of life . . . and fullness of love is accompanied by the blessed thrill of absolute joy."

"Amen I say to you, I do not know you."[8] The bridegroom who would not open the door a crack spoke these words solemnly and with the insistence of solemnity. He did not condemn, nor did he curse them with "Evil women, creatures of vice and iniquity, depart into eternal flames! I disown you!" No, he did not judge. He did not know . . . and that is much more terrifying and definite. Their two worlds did not coincide; they were unaware of each other.

But will somebody contradict our last statement by noting that the foolish virgins knew the bridegroom; they had faith and were eager for heaven . . . and the bridegroom, could he truly not know them? Did he not come to look for them? Does not the Creator know the least of his creatures, and does not the

[8] Mt. 25, 12; Mt. 7, 23; Lk. 13, 25.

redeemer know those souls ransomed by his blood? For we know the divine Bridegroom gave the last drop of his blood for all the foolish virgins just as for the wise. And the wedding feast is this divine life sacrificed to men, shared among men to reanimate and restore them to life forever.

What does "I do not know you" mean? The bridegroom did not say, "I do not love you." Yet the knowledge he meant is the knowledge of love. The bridegroom knew the wise virgins and this knowledge is the spiritual wedding. We truly know in our heart of hearts, when we love, when mutual love results in the mysterious union of the lover and the beloved. It is comprised of superficial knowledge come by meditation on sensible images or abstract ideas, but they do not attain understanding of the intimacy of beings. We would say today that it is not an existential awareness. Raphael said that "To understand we must be equal to the object of our understanding." The ancients thought that only the like could have an awareness of the like. So, for them, visual perception results from the encounter, the harmony, of two ideas. The light in an eye, by the expression which is the exterior projection of it, clashes with light rays emanating from different bodies, becoming united with them, gives us the sensation, the knowledge of forms and colors. Love is the knowledge of minds; love is the light, the rapture of beings encountering one another. The indispensable similarity for deep contact and mutual understanding, is the love of sacrifice, the charity which makes beings receptive to each other. God is Charity. He knows only the souls burning with the charity he diffuses by his Spirit, thanks to the Son's redemption. That is why the loving virgins, on fire with spiritual wisdom, were admitted to the rare knowledge of the divine espousals. That is why the bridegroom did not know the foolish virgins. They were, as the authors of the Middle Ages put it, in the realms of dissimilarity; they lived, according to the same vocabulary, in the love of concupiscence; they understood nothing of the love of charity (*agapē*). Today we would say that the bridegroom and foolish virgins were not on the same wave length. They alone were responsible for their situation. Just as the wise virgins, they could have incorporated in their souls this active and sacrificing generosity, this religion which does not calculate the reward of merits earned, which does not apportion effort, which was not satisfied by the Law, but desired simply to respond to love by love. And since divine love is infinite, this religion is a marvelous round of sacrifices and disinterested excesses.

Love does not know egotism, neither does it recognize moralism—this prideful and legalistic kind of egotism. In that respect, the words of Christ are the expression of an ineluctable necessity against which even pardon can do nothing: besides, a sinner may act on kindly impulses, on bursts of generosity: man is so illogical and so very complex. The Pharisee, true to his breed, cannot have the slightest love without trying to figure out just how much divine Charity will reward him for it.

Therefore, we must be careful to be good with a goodness that does not hope for anything in return before God and our neighbor.[9] We know neither the day nor the hour.[10] At the moment of death it is too late to be generous—too late to love God in our neighbor—too late to be self-sacrificing, and it will

[9] Lk. 12, 35–36.
[10] Mt. 24, 50; 25, 13; Lk. 12, 40.

be too late to lose our ego in his life. Before the face of the God whose name is Charity, it is too late to be foolish with the folly of wisdom. As soon as grace touches your heart, let yourself be filled with the infinite impulse of the soothing goodness which forgets to receive and whose joy is in giving!

The Two Prodigal Sons

LUKE 15, 11–32

THIS is the golden parable, the wonder of wonders. Had someone committed the vilest of sins, and had he once understood
this parable, he would return weeping to the Father. It has accomplished more for the glory of God among men than all the
sermons in the world. It so extravagantly praises the Father's
tender goodness that most of us would be tempted to go along
with the prodigal son on his escapades, it so vividly paints us a
picture of sin's corruption and the virtue which is strengthened
in it. All sinners have called this sentimental and passionate parable of infinite pardon their very own.

And yet it was not told with the express purpose of showing
God's mercy against moral legalism. It is a Gospel commonplace
that the worst is the most interesting and that the child who
causes the most grief is the most loved. All parents and educators can vouch for the truth of this fact by their own experience.
We would hardly dream of analyzing it if it only made up the
first part of a diptych, the thesis of an antithesis whose contrast

would better allow us to grasp a truth which is hidden and quite difficult for all men to grasp!

The Sinner Saved

Here we see a young man who has squandered his part of the inheritance, who lived "life," "his" life. "After all, that's his privilege! Those things belong to him!" In our own day the prodigal son would hardly ruffle the feathers of the proud public leaders who are more or less existentialistic. But when God gives something to his creature, and prior to that when he gave him his very existence, he keeps all things, conserves all things . . . he cannot lose anything: he guards and keeps a loving watch over the destiny of his works; he conserves and maintains in creation that which issued forth from his Being. His hand does not lose its grip over what it offers lest the gift dissolve away into nothingness.

It is in our power to dispose of God's gifts any way we desire, but we do not have the right to do so. These gifts crumble to pieces if we use them wrongly; they may keep us dangerously away from the divine presence, and even though they may be harmless we cannot destroy them, we cannot lose them without doing injury to the Giver's munificence. The children of God must use the goods of this world according to the end for which they were created!

The unruly, and perhaps sophisticated, young man thinks that freedom is license to do all things, even to plunge into dissipation! But in following this line of thought he is actually proclaiming himself a god when he pretends to absolute autonomy —this man who has not even control over his birth, or his death—and is this not sheer blind folly and suicide? The son always needs the father . . . always, and if he runs away from his father, if he shrugs off his father's kindness and paternal authority, if he hides from the awesome authority of his tenderness, he sells himself into the bondage of slavery. Everything he believed to possess turns about and engulfs him. He has nothing whatever. Nothing. He does not count. He is empty and caught up in a terrifying quicksand of his own making.

Vices bloat and puff up with nothingness. The infinite Being alone can give each creature his fullness of being. Vices do not create; they are but magicians playing sleight-of-hand tricks with the empty air. They abandon their victims, leaving them weak, uncertain, drained of their strength. The prodigal son has shaped his desires into false gods, and they, like so many ghouls, have sucked him dry of his substance. The Gospel expresses this quite well: that substance is like a foundation whose destruction provokes the collapse and final fall of the whole structure. God gives us his life and keeps us on our feet. The prodigal son weakened the presence of God within him, and along with that, the honor of God, the splendor of God, the gift of God, by using this fundamental and substantial gift of the Father to his own ends. Nothing more is left to him. When one has sold his God into the darkness, when one has crucified him on the cross of his passions, only the night and the cross remain—the cross standing alone in the night!

The prodigal son, miserable wretch, put his trust in his friends, even those who exploited him and who were just as shallow as himself, chasms of nothingness, shafts of the danaïde.* He put himself into the hands of those who saw only their own ends gained through him, and now since he has nothing more to offer them, he is of no import. His friends slam their door in his face and this is to be expected. When one has no father, he has no brothers!

But the swine do not abandon him. He, alone and forsaken as he would be in hell, sees himself surrounded by pigs. The Jews considered pigs impure, vile animals to be repudiated with disgust, rejected even by God as well as by man, rejected as the personification of sin's corruption of creation. Within the hog-wallow, the prodigal son is worse off than a pig; his soul follows him everywhere and he cannot tear himself away from it. The wings of his spirit, clotted with foul, reeking mud, are motionless and only serve to encumber him. He is envious of the happier lot of the pigs. For the pigs do not go hungry, eating as they do the carobs of the sweet but hollow husks. Pigs can take delight with this hollowness. But the man is burning up with voluptuous appearances, and, in no way satisfied with the void in which they are wrapped, he lives upon his essential hunger. He runs after foods that cannot satisfy the infinite chasm of his craving. The man, in fact, hungers after God alone and can only be filled by God. People in our time, not content with the "earthly foods" littering the world, persist in making of them a "hopeless bondage." Never before have they so masterfully organized the slavery of false happinesses. Beneath the free and joyful soaring

* A water wheel, named after the Danaïdes of Greek mythology who, in punishment for murdering their husbands, were doomed to pour water perpetually into a broken cistern.

of birds intoxicated with the infinite heavens, the pig-like grunt-
ing of the discontent is heard everywhere in the hog-wallow of
the glutted. Famine rages about in this age swarming with
prodigal children and the proliferation of swine.

Return

The miracle of this parable is that the prodigal son "returned
of his own accord." The miracle of grace, the discreet miracle
which is not mentioned, since it goes without saying, because
Christ died for sinners, for their return, for their conversion
which is this turning about, like a glove, from the outside to
the inside. "God has loved us first."[1]

At that very moment the Father was climbing the hill and,
shielding his eyes with his hand, he gazed out over the long
dusty road which spread out from the city. His heart saw further
than his eyes, for it was with his son in the pig-sty so that he
might find it there among the husks . . . and might understand.
Unable to cast off the wings of his soul, the son was equally
unable to uproot his sonship from his flesh. His father's blood
courses powerfully in his arteries and it makes him sad and
prevents him from finding satisfaction with corn husks. This
love which pursues and even precedes him, cuts him off from
animal happiness. In his frightful misery he knows it and is
aware of it and this is the tragic moment, this moment of revolt
from and hatred of this love. It is a revolt which may be conceited and cynical among those especially who are by nature
more stable, and among those who are mediocre it may manifest

[1] 1 Jn. 4, 19.

itself as a larva of revolt in the morass of discouragement, abandonment, in the renunciation of being a man, or quite simply in the renouncement of his existence. As this renouncement is impossible in the anguishing light of God's judgment, this dismal decay, this stupidity, will inevitably give place to a diabolical revolt.

The tragic moment of truth can be the moment of salvation. The prodigal son thus finds himself. He lost himself by dissipation, by bleeding himself dry with pleasure seeking, by the resignation of his personality, eager for inferior goods. He lived a lie. Now he is returning to the truth which demands meditation and the clarity of God, and which lies at the intimate crossroads between the created and the Creator. It is a truth not of reflections but of the creative Light. The son painfully recalls that he is nothing without his Father. In the midst of all his misery he remembers that he has a Father, that he still possesses this extraordinary wealth: a benevolent Being linked to him through goodness. A Father cannot untie the bonds between himself and his son.

The Father's Happiness

Every past happiness, purity, simplicity, and joy unfolds within the heart of the prodigal son. He recalls both the security and intimacy he had with his father, and by contrast, his misery becomes all the more horrible and despicable. The misery of despair! Yet he does not despair. On the contrary, he begins to hope, because both his father's image and love appear infinitely more powerful to him than the image of his downfall. Some people believe that the prodigal son is only then sensibly reasonable. "Am I so foolish as to stagnate in this misery, cast off by all, when all I have to do to regain happiness is to return to my family's farm!" Only faith makes this wisdom possible. It is not enough to dream one's way back on the road of the past and the ideal as do prisoners when they think back on the languid memories of their childhood, their state of innocence, their lessons, the religious instructions of the parish priest, and the example of their parents . . . all those things which preceded that one rash impulse, that fever which set fire to their senses and the folly of pride, when they cut themselves off completely from society, family, Church. . . .

Having searched into himself, the prodigal son finds not his liability, not the simple memory of joys long past, but rather he peers into an eternal truth transcending the vicissitudes of life: his father *is* good, faithfully good. That he was, and that he is still. It is his nature . . . the best proof is that his servants have bread in abundance, now as yesterday and tomorrow: there is always good bread for all those who live and work with him. The prodigal son discovers in the depths of his being that he is always a son, in spite of his sin. His father is always his: "My father!" And this father is always good. This interior revelation and faith in love are essential for hope and therefore essential to the prodigal son's return. No one ever goes back to one whom he knows will slam the door shut in his face.

If we analyze the Gospel text well, we notice that this thought of the offended one's merciful heart precedes that of the sin, precedes that clear awareness of sin which is only possible in the light of love. The prodigal son feels utterly wretched, unsatisfied, already dead. Then, by contrast, he evokes mental images of paternal kindness, source of happiness, fulfillment, life . . . this very kindness he had scoffed. Then he begins to understand the horror of sin which is essentially a form of ingratitude. A blind man is only fully aware of his blindness if he has known the light of day. The prodigal son, at this moment, begins to ache with another pain besides hunger; he begins to suffer his father's hurt. That is why he humbles himself: "I shall arise! [Yes, I'll have the courage! I shall once again walk with my head held high.] I shall go to my father and say, 'My Father, I have sinned against heaven and against you (against your commandments, against the order of creation . . . but especially against your person, against your heart!). I am no longer worthy to be called your son; treat me as one of your slaves . . . (which you treat as beloved servants)!' "[2] His father is always good, he is always "his" father. He was unworthy, he did not behave as a son and he no longer wanted to recognize this honor and advantage. As if it were possible! If the father remains truly the father, the son will watch for every opportunity: he remains a son. But the new humility of the prodigal son tells him to stay put on the level of justice, and it seems quite just for him to be received as a slave after having fled as a son. As humiliating as it may be, this degradation would be merciful enough. Absolute justice is the result of the deserter's act: the pig-sty forever.

Wallowing in shame, the prodigal son imagines that he has arisen, admitted his error, that he is humbled and that upon returning home he has eaten to satiety. He foresees what meeting his father would be like. And it is a powerful idea. This dream

[2] Lk. 15, 21.

97

and hope are like a lock suddenly springing open. One day he will recall that he got up, set off, and that he had gone a great distance. Between sin and grace. In proportion as he goes his way, his sin weighs more and more heavily upon him as though it had been transformed into a millstone; his father's face seems increasingly sad, perhaps even wrathful. Was he right to count on love more than justice? Panic takes hold of him. But he can retreat no longer, and before him there surely awaits some bread as good as his father's heart. The prodigal son continues his adventurous journey, repeating his confession over and over to himself.

"My Father!" I shall call him: "My Father . . ." Ah! the use of sentiment! This gives him back some lost confidence. . . . "I am not worthy . . ." Neither did the centurion feel worthy that Christ should enter into his house, this house where sickness typifies sin.[3] Sin is with the prodigal son on his homeward journey and it is this which dares ask to take possession of his father's house. But we all know that sin has no traffic with holiness. To re-become a son he must be transfigured or nothing is possible (without a transfiguration communion would be a sacrilegious parody). The sinner does not reflect on that; he remains on a prosaic mercenary level. He is too concerned with not going hungry and not enough concerned about regaining a warm life of tenderness with the one he has betrayed. He stays fixed on a level of fear, and his outlook is still a negative, not a positive, overture. He does not see evil, misery, darkness any-more—that is certain—he wishes to remain a slave, his Father's slave, of course, and no longer slave to the idols of vice, but he

[3] Mt. 8, 8.

98

still is a slave all the same. "Freedom," he thinks, "I have long enough desired! But I understood. . . . A booby-trap! A device to increase your hunger, to turn you into a pig." I do not know whether or not he was familiar with the story of Ulysses and Circe. But his was a slave's mentality. "A slave I shall remain. That is all I deserve! I am no longer capable of directing myself alone. I shall exchange this cherished freedom which has been so harmful to me, for a piece of bread, bought with the very thing I renounced for it." It is never necessary to renounce this freedom. Without it there is no love. He does not know it. Nevertheless he has already risen and begun his journey; he has already chosen his father, or rather his father's bread. But what is the difference between God and his kindness?

The Father's Love

As an individual he no longer matters. His father did not send the police to bring him back: he was not worth the trouble. "This fool," he dreams, "will return more miserable and more submissive to his original way of life, or else he will die of thirst in the desert." It did not occur to him that this fool believed in pardon and was going to his father!

The prodigal son is of more worth to his father, he counts more now than ever before; nothing matters more than him! He has great need of him; his life is endangered, a gaping hole is in his heart; half of his soul has gone from him and the other half is dying because of it. He lives now in expectancy of the return, the healing of the wound, the full recovery of his love and life. If one reverses the relation, he somewhat resembles his lost son. His son left, obsessed by another happiness he did not have, which he lacked and which unfortunately was only a false happiness. Happiness is interior—in the palm of your hand —at home. We are so used to it that we do not see it. We find it a normal, uninteresting thing with no value; we pay it no attention or interest. When this happiness is lost, then we discover the cost, but is too late! The son lost the father; the father lost the son. In the end it makes no difference that one is guilty and the other not: both are unhappy. The innocent always suffer the mistakes of the guilty; he is victim and pledged to bring him back, to pay for his salvation. Deprived of each other, the father and son are found more closely united than ever before . . . and the repenting prodigal son begins to know his father's grief just as his father suffers his. They must at all costs find themselves, father and son, before they can hope to find their happiness, their true happiness. The father is not averse to freedom. When his son decided to leave him, he wept over it, but he did not force him to remain. He did not send armed men to compel him to return home. He waits until his son returns to him of his own free will where his love keeps watch and lets the mysterious inner summons do its work in his son's heart. He wants no slave. He wants his son. And his love reaches fever pitch to the extent that he senses within himself a presentiment of his son's return, and then he rushes out to meet the one whom he knew in his heart was approaching. Suddenly, deep within himself he knows that he is fulfilled and that there is an answer to his summons. . . .

"But while he was yet a long way off, his father saw him and was moved with compassion, and ran and fell upon his neck and kissed him."[4] He does not see his son's sin, but rather his misfortune, his sorrowful downfall—he sees only the worn-out man, staggering, in rags, who, weeping, cries out to him: "Father, I have sinned against heaven and before you. I am no longer worthy to be called your son."[5] Such is his prepared confession; but already he has changed, transformed, completely modified his words. On the way home he admitted he was not worthy to be his son; but in his father's arms he learns that he is always his son in spite of what he has done, or even because of everything, and he says: "I am no longer worthy to be called your son."[6] He does not add: "Treat me as one of your slaves!" For the father is master; he knows what he has got to do; and he calls him once more his son. Now, *to call* in Hebrew is the same word as *to create*. The father re-creates or revives his son —the very same one who was dead!

It would be quite just if the father did not ask his son's pardon for not having shown him the excess of his love earlier. "He would not have thought of leaving home!" But this is no time for regret; joy rings out vibrantly—a paschal joy! The prodigal son can only embrace him. By now the servants are laying out the white robe for him to wear—the robe of the faithful sons. Once again he is pure and cleansed of all sin—sin which is separation that radically destroys the grace of union. "Place a ring on his finger!" The ring typifies the freely renewed bond, the chosen dependence which is not servitude, but is filiation. "Give him sandals for his feet!" Sandals to walk, to cover great

---

[4] Lk. 15, 20.
[5] Lk. 15, 21.
[6] Lk. 15, 21.

distances in the best of conditions. Love has no limits. An ideal future is placed before the feet of the son who has the infinite ahead of him.

Restored to his dignity and true freedom, the son at that moment sees the arrival of the fatted calf to be used for sacrifice. The father wisely thought his son would truly appreciate the perfect robe, the ring, and the sandals with a full stomach. The son is going to appease his hunger—the boundless hunger of joy. The father also is faring well because of his new-born happiness. The feast of the lost son found again begins amid the rejoicing of fifes and trumpets and tambourines.

The Faithful Son Condemned

However, there is someone who shuns this rejoicing: the elder brother who only enters the parable at the very end in order to give it full meaning—to complete Christ's message. Jesus, in speaking of the prodigal son, did not wish mainly to exalt God's mercy. He directed his words to another truth which rises up out of the contrast between the prodigal son rewarded and the faithful son dissatisfied. It is an incomprehensible scene which begins to unfold here—a scene we would like prudently to avoid to spare ourselves the unseemliness of pointing out a gaping discrepancy between the two sons' treatment by their father. Up to this point we would approve of the parable. But is it a just and reasonable pardon that demands the sinner be received triumphantly? But we never know! We can quite easily become prodigal children ourselves—who of us has nothing to be reproached for? which of us has never betrayed? The wonderful reception of the guilty—the total forgiving—that, all things considered, is reassuring enough for us—and makes us tolerant of others.

Nevertheless, how can we not look favorably upon the elder son? He served his father without ever transgressing his orders. Now, the father forgets his loyalty, and what is worse, speaks reproachfully to him. Such a lack of tact and flagrant injustice disturbs and ruins the good impression of a generous pardon. We are outraged. It seems fitting to remain protected within the festive clamor, within the intoxicating cover of merry-making, and bring the parable to a fine conclusion with the entrance of the fatted calf—to cut the text at this point and not think of the scandal which follows. To be kind, let us say the foolish joy of the father was responsible for his awkward and shocking inexpediency which ensues.

It is only a short step from that to forget about the first-born son. We admire him, say his is the perfect workman—not a reveller, sure of himself, prompt, so faithful that no one ever imagines him as one tempted with evil desires—and we register him in the catalogue of virtue and, piously, there we leave him. We may ask ourselves whether his father ever worried about him. Does he who never causes anxiety count? We keep him transfixed on the unchanging scene of nature—in the fields—, in this happy stability, where, by force of habit, there is no longer any awareness, and this allows him to set out upon a dangerous course unchecked. Does the father, who thinks only of the prodigal son, have any room in his mind for the elder son?

But here the music rings out; if there are no fireworks, there is still quite a lot of noise nonetheless. The elder son listens hard.

103

"There is nothing to celebrate! It comes from our home. What's going on there?" The sun is flush on the horizon as he comes back from a long, long day of hard work. He wipes the sweat off his forehead, cleans up his tools and hastens to the house to see what is going on. His curiosity ever increases. "They're certainly having a good time! Why didn't they tell me about it?" Now he hears the voices of the guests, their songs and laughter. He sees the busy servants going out and coming in. He calls out to one of them. "What's this all about?"—"What? You don't know? But your brother, the reveller, he's come back, not gloriously, but in good health all the same. He has come back in time. Your father is mad with joy over the whole thing and he has killed the fatted calf." Hearing this, the virtuous son feels the earth buckle up under him as his heart leaps to his throat. He becomes livid with rage. "The fatted calf," he stammers, "and for him!" Perhaps he had his eye on the fatted calf? At least he thought about his brother—but not kindly. He judged his brother by his acts, quitting work, leaving his father and making him suffer. It was best not to speak of him, to wipe him out of his heart and memory. The first-born son had conditioned his soul so well that it had become a rock of contempt, and he took a certain delight in "not being that kind of man as his brother," and he completed his transformation by hoarding up the dullness of oblivion about his brother. And now the vagabond brother and reveller breaks through this silence, this interior peace, to rise up in the joy of tambourines and flutes. He was buried in his heart and now he rises triumphantly, not as a memory, but as a looming presence. It would be enough to go into the feast to see him with his father, reunited in love. But he is too angry. His world of values, his ideas about the economy of creation are shattered and he does not admit it. He had his own idea about morality, justice, his own idea of life, and he believed himself in complete harmony with his father. But by a secret progress of sentiments and facts, one inconceivable thing flashes through his mind: he is outside and the prodigal son is within—in his father's house! Abashed, he learns that the sinner has the lot of the just man and the just man is rebuked. A sickening fate to be sure, yet less disgusting than his father's sudden injustice. Then . . . then the sinner deserved grace more than the saint? Virtue remains on the threshold, astonished at becoming evil in the eyes of the father, an evil which his goodness must redeem and save. The elder brother has become the new prodigal son.

The Father's Mind

"Come on in!", said the servant with an air of artless simplicity. But such an act would seem to the elder son the acceptance of unfairness. He prefers to call aloud at the door so that only his protest might enter into the feast. In the meanwhile the servant informs the master, "Your other son is there behind the door, and he's furious!" The father, apprehensive, arises at once. Is he going to lose this son because of the prodigal's return? He is not content with saying, "Let him enter! I shall explain to him . . ." No! The father's love is always the first—it takes the initiative. As he was on the road in advance of the prodigal son, so he is in going to meet the elder son. He begs him to join in the feasting. Humbly, fondly. Perhaps he imagines the excess of happiness has made him forget the elder son whom he should have told as soon as possible. Might it be that he said he was tactless? "Come! Enter! You understand: I was carried away with my joy. I only thought of him, of his return at last! He's alive and filled with love! He is there! Come in: he will be delighted to see you once again!" Personally, we do not believe that the father, tactless as he might seem to us, had forgotten his eldest son. Nor do we believe that the Father would have had to make excuses and that he was effectively excused. He explains, but he does not excuse: he invites his "faithful" son who is outside just as Christ died outside the walls of Jerusalem to touch the sinner's heart.

We are always tempted to fill our exegeses with the mentality of the elder brother, and, within the framework of this system of judgments and feelings, the father is guilty; with kindness, we add as soon as the circumstances merit our attention and we are satisfied that he acted by running ahead of the righteously offended brother. We assent, almost by instinct, to the bitter words tumbling from his lips still trembling with rage: "Behold, these many years I have been serving you, and have never transgressed one of your commands; and yet you have never given me a kid that I might make merry with my friends. But when this your son comes, who has devoured his means with harlots, you killed for him the fatted calf."[7] These words stun the father. A moment's carelessness throws light on an inad-

[7] Lk. 15, 30.

106

missible conduct. The ungrateful father did not love his faithful, obedient, hard-working son. Lack of justice comes from an empty heart. The father favored his second son and, in spite of his shortcomings, he always loved him and was prepared to forgive him everything. This is a weak father, a poor simple-minded father of little character. The entire parable of the prodigal son turns out tainted, dissipated by this arduous contestation. What a pity the divine narrator did not end with the fatted calf!

Yet the divine story teller, without making his illustration acceptable at the expense of a simple account that would only accord an important place to human reason, wanted to disturb us in order to revolutionize our minds. He grasps our thought between the two forks of a wicked-looking pair of tongs: on one hand we are bewildered—"against him"—and on the other hand we believe in him, trusting his word. If faith is the stronger, then it must of necessity disrupt our thinking and shape it like his own.

At the door of the house, outside the joyous feasting, a drama takes place whose outcome we do not know, as though we ourselves were actually the faithful sons, as though we were intimately concerned in the plot, and as though it were up to us to give the parable a joyous or sad conclusion. The tragic dialogue presents us with the elements of the problem and it is up to us to figure out whether we are on the side of the misunderstood son's logic or on that of the incomprehensible father. To stress this dramatic character, the elder is no longer presented as a son: "Your son is he who has devoured all your goods . . . I, I have increased them—I have done that—and without me you would only have fallow ground! I have never been your son, never! You want proof? You have never rewarded me. Not even a kid have you allotted me! No, I did not dream of having the fatted calf, but a kid would have given me such a great pleasure, and that much you have refused me!"

The father answers with such power of persuasion when he begs him to enter, that we are tempted to ask ourselves just where we stand, where the truth lies. We think of it as a misunderstanding, like a conversation between two deaf men. Yet we must recognize that from the very outset the father has been winning ground. If he was culpable, it was an unconscious sort of guilt: he did not hesitate for an instant; he is clear; pure; he has always loved his faithful son; and he still loves him. Not once did he rebuke him. But he reproached him gently to help him along towards the hoped-for conversion of his heart: the distraught son must enter into the joy of his father's house.

"My child!" With the very first word he strikes right into the heart of the matter. "You, you indeed are my son. In your anger you tell me that you are not and even that you never have been, that I have only looked upon you as a slave. What a distortion! You are my child." He chose the softest word. He did not say "You are my first-born!" but "You are my little child. My other son rebelled against me yesterday, and now, today, it is you who make me suffer, you, my favored one." He said "my child" to this hot-tempered man uttering bitter words for the first time and without having preceded them, as the prodigal son, with the wonderful words, "My Father!" Now, "child" means someone who does not speak. A tiny child is capable of great fits of anger, but he has no reason. The father considers those words hurled at him as the little instinctive rage of a child that has no weight and not much importance. For such children the father's wisdom is folly or scandal . . . and for him, his children's wisdom is an empty logic.

Let us listen to the father's logic: "Son, you are always with me, and all that is mine is yours; but we were bound to make merry and rejoice, for this your brother was dead, and has come to life; he was lost and is found."[8] These words resemble those which were told to the workers of the first hour: "Are you envious because I am generous?"[9] "I am good and I pardon! But I am not unjust. What is all this about the kid, when all that I possess is yours!" The father has always been a father loving both the prodigal and the faithful son.

The Self-Righteous Son

But after all, what did the fidelity of the elder son consist of? The value of actions and behavior is interior. Outwardly, the elder son is the perfect son. Interiorly, he is also a prodigal son, and perhaps more gravely so than the other, in a way which is cheaper, more shameful, more calculating, more selfish, and in any event more deceitful. One sinned frankly, openly, but in the depths of his soul there still was an aching loyalty, scorned, rejected, but still alive, which could accept the grace necessary

[8] Lk. 15, 31.
[9] Mt. 20, 15.

for the return, a grace comparable to a seed which dies, but comes to life once again. . . . The other son wore virtue as a façade. He led a devoted life, showed visible honesty; but his intention was not right. There was no more life in him; the elder son is no longer a son, but a Pharisee! Had he been a true son, he would have suffered the absence of the prodigal son, he would have watched for his return just as the father did; he would not have lived for his base interests in his father's fields; he would not have wanted to be rich, doubly rich, rich without having to share his wealth. Had he been a true son, he would have been a true brother; with the same heart as his father he would have run up to the returning youth and he would have cried out his joy in embracing him and he would have told his father: "Kill the fatted calf." The elder son was not there to greet his brother because he had no love for him: his heart was elsewhere; his heart did not beat in unison with his father's. That is why the father did not excuse himself for not having invited him: he ought not to be absent. If the father's heart had been most of all concerned with the fields, the first part of this parable would have been impossible!

"What is she doing here?", complained the angered "faithful" countrymen when a famous French comedienne came to Mass for the first time. "There she is!" Very many Christians have taken their religion to be a rationalistic moral system of the eighteenth century. But Christ's religion is a mystical one, and it is a love which gives morality its limits and its meaning; it gives it a soul and a vivifying spirit. Neither formalism nor human wisdom are the Gospel. For the letter kills and what

Christ brings out in his mysterious parable is life. Let us take care to detach ourselves from the elder son whom we understand only to well, to our condemnation.

The elder son has a moral system; that does not mean he loves the good that he does. Prudence keeps him from doing evil: he needs the kingdom of his father, his heaven. He is no man's fool: he wants to lose nothing! Therefore, he made up his mind to do his work: he will not leave the father. Not out of love for his father. But to insure his own happiness. He knows vice only gives quickly passing pleasures that immediately give way to sorrow and misery. If he could just go out on a little debauch and feast upon a kid! But his father concedes him nothing—and he can grant no such thing, for love does not destroy the morality it surpasses, and the least sin remains a sin, inadmissible, forbidden, eternally forbidden. The submissive son has borne this servitude of virtue heavily, dreading the slightest indiscretions which lead to greater ones, not wanting almighty God, not wanting to lose his paradise for a folly. The prodigal son is a fool! But not he! He knew too well how to sacrifice the present for the future. He is solidly reasonable.

He is totally unable to understand his father, his folly of forgiving. It exasperates him, it throws him into a rage which is as the despairing cry of a life come to nothing—a failure. What good is virtue if the sinner is feted, if they forget his offense, if they reëstablish him to his inheritance? The elder brother— he also—regrets that he has not profited from his life. He struggled along for nothing, was mortified and sacrificed for nothing. He is allowed nothing, and he indulges in nothing.

111

His brother is given everything; the result is the same. More-over, the sinner is better treated than he with all his virtue! In its painful existence with the faithful son, the comfortable thought of his father's curse dumfounding the guilty one has always been a powerful helpmate in his moral struggle; he de-lighted in justice. He gloated over the refusal of the father at the cost of concubinage with swine. He did not think the faithful love of the father was always the last chance for his son, even a prodigal son, even though he be dreadfully guilty of sinning (for there is no question of whitewashing the sins com-mitted). That this wretch, his brother, snatches ahold of it, is for him the most ghastly of catastrophes—the death of his reason for living.

He claims to be victim of injustice, for he supposes at heart, as did the prodigal son, there can be no happiness without a complete severing off from his father, without freedom from morality, in allowing himself the company of friends, and then courtesans, in going to eat the kid first and the pork later. But happiness is not in the fat of the calf ceremoniously immolated. Happiness is to be with the father; heaven is to communicate love, to be nourished with the joy of shared love. To be loved, everything is there, and in this love, everything which one member has is for the other, not by possession or by authority of one over the goods which the other leaves him, but by a mutual generosity, by the entire gift of one to the other. That is why those who are in love suffer together, hope together, are devoted together, pardon together, and rejoice together! The elder brother, who only lived for himself, who made the moral order into a ticket for paradise, a right to happiness, not only did he not suffer the father's grief at the prodigal's flight, his misery and damnation, but he rejoiced over it. His brother. He killed him within his heart and he hoped against his resurrection. He is still opposed to it. No! He will not enter; he will not admit this law of love which remains exterior. Now he lives outside the realm of love. For this reason the father left the banquet hall to try and save him, but the healing of Pharisees is the most difficult kind for they proudly believe themselves to be living incarnations of virtue. The elder son's words are the same as those words making up the prayer of the Pharisee.

True Fidelity

How often Christians do not know what their happiness is, they who cast longing eyes towards some evil which they do not commit because they love themselves too much! They have the grace of baptism: God lives in them; with them . . . and for them this fact is not an ecstasy and the whole of their life. They fall back from this presence as from a cross on the earthly road. The sorry work, the drudgery of being faithful. They little stop to think that this happiness which they wish to buy with the help of merits is precisely to be with God forever, to see him eternally. They do not imagine that because of grace, heaven, happiness, is already in them. They do not know it because they do not truly love. . . . They hope for heaven to be like the heaven of Mohammed!

God would tell them—but at the gate of heaven—and would

113

they ever understand: "You did not love me when I was with you. Regulation only has meaning through love; the Law has no value without charity. You are like sounding brass! You are nothing, and deserving of nothingness!" It is possible that the rejected, on the threshold of night, will protest as in the parable of the last judgment (all the parables are of the same spirit, the same light, like stars clustered together in the Milky Way, the royal road to salvation). Thus it is possible that the condemned souls will protest: "How can I not have loved you—I, who have always been faithful to you?"[10] The answer is only too clear: "All that you neglected to do for your brother, you have not done for me. Because your heart is removed from your brother, it is cut off from mine; for I loved him and you should have loved him with me. You have not accepted him; you spurned my invitations; since you have refused to enter and restore your heart to your brother, you are no longer my son and I know you not. Remain outside where there will be weeping and gnashing of teeth, the hell of jealousy and hatred. . . ."

Let us be careful not to forget that love of our neighbor is inseparably linked to the love of God, that he is a type of it, the revealer of it. It is hard to understand Christians discussing the salvation of the workers at the eleventh hour and the converts at the last minute! They do not digest the happiness of others which seems stolen from them! Still, in charity, they would be able to say: "So much the better for them!" The saddest thing about them, we insist, is to learn through their conversations that they do not already have this joy, that God is in them as a dead

[10] Mt. 25, 44.

114

God, and God's heavy sarcophagus weighs upon their lives . . . and that is all. They do not dream of being thankful that God, from the beginning, has given them the privilege of his love. Had they understood the gift of God, they would rejoice for having daily borne the suffering of God, for having been sacrificed with him for their brothers, for having transfigured the moral order in charity and obedience to the law in an exemplary apostolate, in a self-immolation for their neighbor. "Happy they who dwell in your house! Continually they praise you!"[11] For there is no truer fidelity than the heart's. . . . And they who are unselfishly faithful, who love both the Father of heaven and their earthly brothers, they have happiness here below. They did not look for happiness, but only for love, and happiness is given them in abundance, on the same cross.

In the meanwhile, the prodigal son, having returned to the source of love, sighs painfully, as did his brother St. Augustine: *Domine, sero te amavi!* Lord, late have I loved you!

[11] Ps. 84 (83), 5.

The Barren Fig Tree

LUKE 13, 6–9

THIS parable, just as that of the vine-dressers, has been interpreted in the historical sense. The man coming to look for fruit on his fig tree in the middle of his vineyard is God visiting Israel and waiting for the Chosen People's repentance and fidelity. The vine-dresser is Christ who for three years continued to nurse the barren tree in the hope that it might produce some fruit. The threat, unfortunately, which overhangs the fig tree, will be realized because the efforts of the Saviour will have been in vain: Jerusalem will be razed by Titus, the tree will be hacked down.

The Ineluctable Law

It would be superfluous for us to reiterate what we said earlier about the spiritual sense of history when we discussed the parable of the vine-dressers. But, because of our subject of legalism or ritualism in the psychological evolution of the individual, it would not appear useless to stress this point once again. It shows up in the evolution of peoples who have reached their mental age. Ritualism characterizes a civilization which considers exterior things as essential; it is there from the outset. Moralism characterizes the age of reason. It is not surprising to find that the century which produced the encyclopedists valued duty over love: parish priests as the guardians of human wisdom, fell into this error; they slighted the beatitudes and harped on the ten commandments. The God of love preaching the folly of the cross is eclipsed by an abstract and authoritarian rule . . . the return to the Law! There is much more to be appreciated in the scheme—the summary—of the stages of humanity's growth as proposed by Auguste Comte. This philosopher seems to lack a deep notion of the hierarchy of values, the intemporal hierarchy of artistic genius or the spirit of saintliness which, such as the intellect, can overpower individualities of any age and culture and assume them. Now in the life of an individual we can likewise discover those periods which are naturally more receptive to ritual, to mystic morals, which acknowledge that the spiritual, in any epoch, can be manifested with splendor. However, the saintly child and adult differ in the expression of their sanctity by as much as St. Jean-Marie Vianney differs from St. Thomas Aquinas!

Having seen this, it is much easier to admit that human existence passes through different phases of development either more Judaical or more Christian. A seven-year-old child may live in the fresh poetry of love: he speaks easily with God whom he imagines with an imagination barely stamped with the seal of reality. A ten year old is more positive: and so, in the Mass his piety consists in serving well, and if he is in choir, it consists in not striking a false note. A fourteen year old, caught in the agony of sin, awakens to a spirituality of fear and aspires to love as to a protection. It is the same with adults . . . without speaking of the various social melieux predisposing individuals to legalism or revolution, to conservatism or progress, etc. It is fortunate that psychologists and religious educators bear in mind the important substratum of normal comportment!

The Law's Sterility

There are rhythms of life and Judaism is one ineluctable spiritual phase by the fact that at the outset everything centers around the preservation of the life of the individual, and also because a certain natural egotism is preliminary. On the other hand, the existence of sin is a fact, and man, from birth, arises to meet his destiny with this particular knife stuck in his back. It would be a mistake to believe that Judaism belongs to ancient history, and that after Christ, the Israelite morality in us was removed through baptism. St. Augustine understood this and wrote of it in his treatise *De Spiritu et Littera*. This is one stage which we all must go through, but we have got to advance beyond it, or otherwise the Israelite becomes the Pharisee. If the Law is receptive to love, then it will be justified: sap needs the whole network of woody fibres to do what it must. St. Bernard tells us what he thinks are the gradations of spiritual ascension: love of self for self; love of God for self; love of God for God; love of self for God. No one can overcome himself easily and no stage of the interior life is harmful if it is a preparation to a higher stage. We recall having once seen a desk of wrought iron which was attributed to an early genius. It was in the chapter room

118

of Citeaux, and it represents a monk freeing himself from vices and gradually ascending, carrying with him a bunch of grapes that increase in size and weight until they are presented to the Virgin, to Christ, to the Trinity.

We, in our parable, are also concerned with a question of fruit. God visits his vineyard and draws near the barren fig tree. He examines Israel to find some fruit ripening, or at least beginning to bud; he wants to see charity coming into blossom; he wishes to gather the fruit for eternity. As we have seen before in the introduction, while drawing attention to the fig tree in the vineyard, the parable invites us to an exegesis geared towards the history of the individual soul, the fig tree, in the vineyard which is humanity. In this way we are able to distinguish this parable from those of the prophets where the vineyard which produces only verjuice is Israel condemned.[1]

Every personal destiny has universal repercussion. The vineyard and fig tree are interdependent: and scientists who have studied Palestinian gardens affirm this fact! The fig tree plays an important role in the shade it brings over the vineyard and in the protection it affords the twisting young vineshoots. But, helpful as the tree is, it needs food: its roots vie with the rest of the vineyard for subsistence, and if the tree is barren, its presence is not only undesirable, but it is detrimental as well. If creatures of the second spiritual category do no good, they at least cause no harm. The more important of them are called to greater works. They think: "We are not evil. We exist, nothing more, and we wish nothing from anyone." They are not aware that they exhaust good soil for their own existence. How often it is

[1] Is. 5, 1–7; 27, 2–6. See Ez. 17, 1–10; 15, 1–8.

119

we meet pseudo-Christians, complacent in their "legalism," not understanding at all that their strict egotism, though lacking harshness and ill-will, is nevertheless a harmful plague: they not only do not benefit from the devotion necessary to the law of charity; but under the surface they are debasing, exploiting their environment because of their basic principles and their roots.

Therefore, the fig tree is to be held accountable, for it is an individual living off others and giving nothing to God. It lives alone and for itself. It must be salvaged at any cost both for itself, for others . . . and for God! If, as we shall see, the pedagogy of salvation requires man's collaboration, it is first of all the work of grace. Certainly, our parable does not go so far as to confound Christ with the tree—fig tree or vineyard, what is the difference![2] The aspect of actual grace or providence is more obvious than sanctifying grace. But it is a fact that, evil being at the root of all our activity after the fall, our action alone is powerless to purify itself. Without love, the fig tree is incapable of giving itself, of loving. It must be brought back to life with a new sap. The feverish activity of Christ the Gardener who digs around the tree and fertilizes it indicates a pervasive, communicating will desirous of passing his generosity into this creature who lives, as it were, in a vacuum. Our Lord's grace goes to the extreme of sacrifice, to the limit of the possible, which the number of perfection, three, symbolizes. Three years means to the ultimate limit, and one year over that besides—all the result of a foolishly excessive outpouring of love—which led Christ to be scourged, despised, crucified! Every man, especially

[2] See Jn. 15, 1–8: allegory of the vine and the branches.

if he is given charge of souls (and who of us is entirely free
from this responsibility?), is therefore the object of God's ineffable patience.

Love Rising Out of Love

Here we are not concerned with exhorting sinners to patience
—though it is a most praiseworthy imitation of God! Nor is it
a question of, as some maintain because of all the gardener's
digging and fertilizing, an exhortation to penitence . . . for it is
Jesus, the vine-dresser, to whom the evil is given and upon whom
the duty falls to perform the penance for the sake of the selfish
fig tree. This is an exhortation to love. Without a doubt love
shows through in God's patience, in the unflagging will of the
redeemer. Love is manifested in a deep and meaningful act: the
divine Workman toils for each individual soul, cutting away evil
influences, nourishing it with a rich spiritual food . . . but above
all he respects its individuality. Grace is offered, never imposed.
It is all around and at the roots as well. Grace is never forced.
Love is freely offered.

God's love encourages us to love. The fig tree has the last
word in the matter. It must accept. It must accept not only
because God's love is given, as minerals in the earth, to aid its
growth and the sheen of its foliage, but also in order to bear
fruit, to love itself in giving itself. It would be a sacrilegious
legalism to seem to obey, to seem to pose as a plant blessed by
God, to pose as a shameless beneficiary in the Lord's blood.
This would be tantamount to embracing in a hideous death
grip the selfless life which is immolated from loving too much.
As the object of such a folly, the fig tree also oversteps the bounds

121

of human wisdom. If it accepts, it will be covered with blossoms and will feed upon the fruits offered, offered first of all by the hand of God. There is nothing more important, nothing more wonderful than the quickening of a soul to charity. Each fruit is a sign of life as it is the happy result of life. There are even signs of this to be found in nature. Thus, the seed is meant to grow; it is great with what it is given, fresh, joyful, and strong. The sun is only magnificent because its rays shoot out extravagantly from its source. The seed and the sun are but feeble images of the real generation: the truly living beget and are not lessened by it; other beings grow up round about them. (The Hebrews considered fertility a heavenly blessing, and barrenness a curse.) The fruits of animal or vegetable life are but faint images of the fruits of the intellect: thought which gives of itself unstintingly. Love, fruit of the spirit, is more noble than thought. The more a being is lifted up into being, the more it is given; the more a being is spiritualized, the more it loves. The barren fig tree, despite its appearance, is dead, and we know it, dead to others, dead to itself, dried up, good only for the fire where glittering appearances are but ashes and dust: *Memento, homo . . . !*

Every fruit is as a child born from its mother's womb, a new entity, a creation meant for others: it is born to be harvested, eaten, or sold. The tree gives itself, but only through the mediation of its fruit. But, only if it accepts separation and sacrifice can this mediation be achieved. This fruit given, this surplus of self, this charity present and presented, is what our Lord awaits from us. He waits not so much for our rational adoration, as he does the attitude of a soul living until death to nourish other souls, according to the Holy Spirit: in this way the glory due to the Father is given back to him: the glory of Charity.

We may imagine a conversation between the good fig tree and the good vine-dresser. In this conversation we may think of the fig tree calling the vine-dresser, beseeching him to dig around its trunk and to bring in some fertilizer. May our freedom imitate his! God does not need us and we have so great a need of him to break away from our envious greed, to open us up to the fullness of creation. That this God who can be removed from our hearts, begs us to try to love, is proof that true love is utterly disinterested, but also that there truly is a community, a pleroma, in which this love can be held in check. Otherwise creation would never reach its fullness. What a formidable mystery!

St. Matthew gives us the complementary anecdote of the cursed fig tree—which is an "active"[3] parable. There is no danger in St. Luke's parable; the danger in St. Matthew's comes to pass. When God declares the time for harvest, the fig tree has only its leaves to show. The demands of charity lie in God's good time and as he desires. But the die is cast. The will diabolically rebels and is struck with eternal death. "And immediately the fig tree dried up."

The tree of life stands facing the cursed fig tree. And its fruit no longer is the love of man for God, but love of God for man. Creation, redemption: the creation of beings outside the Being, salvation or renovation of these beings in Being, what greater superabundance than the Trinity's which is not closed up within itself in its perfect interchange, but because of an unthinkable

[3] Mt. 21, 18–22.

increase of love, is made the fruit of man! We, by a legitimate turning from this parable, and because the spiritual life forms the cycle of God to man and of man to God, we may end here with a prayer of hope: May the man who passes unavoidably into a phase of soul-less ritualism or selfish moralism, may the man of the Law not shut himself off in this Pharisaism, but let him be made receptive to Charity! May he harvest this fruit of the Infinite, as the master or vine-dresser at the foot of the fig tree, by patience and sacrifice, with his hand held open to receive this love as a food which is communion! Such is the wisdom of salvation!

The Good Samaritan

LUKE 10, 25–37

THIS is one of the outstanding parables. The peristyle attests it: "Master, what must I do to gain eternal life?"[1] the doctor of the Law asks the Lord of Charity. From the very outset, the moral law and religion confront each other.

Christ answers him according to the Law, for the Law also teaches love: it says that it is "reasonable" to respond to God's love with our own, provided we give him our whole heart, soul, and strength—provided that we give our whole being, and not haggle over how much we have to give. Therein lies wisdom. We have received all things, we owe everything. The Law is simple and peremptory: we must love. That is the way it is; that is the order. Just as love "does not command," and requires a free will, a spontaneous outpouring, the Gospel assumes and spiritualizes the Law: Christ on the cross excites us to love and by the excess of his sacrifice creates the response and the bestowal of the creatures who "choose" him.

[1] Lk. 10, 25.

125

Our True Neighbor

The Law also adds: "Love your neighbor as yourself!"[2] This is less clearly seen: unless, according to the way the doctor of the Law understood it, your neighbor is a relative of the same race. But our Lord does not understand it in this way, and when, to confuse him and justify himself by perplexing him, the doctor asks: "Who is my neighbor?", the answer is such as to make the sectarian Jews bristle, for our neighbor is not the man who came down from Jerusalem to Jericho and was assailed by robbers; our neighbor is not the poor, the sick, the unfortunate, or even the sinner who is the quintessence of misfortune. Yet all sermons say so with a touching conviction that softens tender hearts— which just goes to show the traditional carelessness of preachers with regard to the sacred texts. True, we must love those who suffer, those victims of life and the Prince of Darkness if we are to save them. However, this is not the direct teaching of the parable of the good Samaritan. Now, the good Samaritan is our neighbor whom we must love!

As a matter of fact, having described the selfish indifference of the priest, Levite, and all who, having seen the victim, passed him by, and after having stressed the willing and lasting devotion of the Samaritan, our Lord asks the doctor—as though consulting him, "Which of these three, in your opinion, proved himself neighbor to him who fell among the robbers?"[3] And the doctor's reply was not: "None, but the injured and the robbed Jew." He spoke as though it were obvious: "He who

[2] Lk. 10, 27.
[3] Lk. 10, 36.

took pity on him!"[4] —Yes, this man is not "estranged," but "drawn close" to the unfortunate fellow lying half dead on the roadside; he took him and placed him on his own beast: he became his neighbor! Such a man as that we must love, and to the beneficiary of his help we owe recognition. Nobody can find fault with that, or be astonished at seeing a "doctor" discovering it alone. This learned man did not speak proudly—as though it were easy to love one's neighbor if it is the right thing to do, or to see him because it is good.

After the doctor had slipped out of the crowd and found himself alone, he surely angrily reproached himself, for the Lord had, if we may use the expression, "possessed" him. He was carried away by his logic and the Lord deceived him into declaring—and in public—that we must love our "enemies"! He, disgraced forever, a Judaean-born Jew, clean among the clean, wise among the wise, had concluded with Christ, or rather even ahead of Christ, that he had the obligation to love the unclean, the uneducated, the Samaritans! Up to that time the commentators of the Law had seen their neighbor as a compatriot, at least a proselyte, a friend of the Jews. And now this innovator comes along breaking down barriers, spreading the seeds of internationalism. . . .

Imagine, if you will, a sermon like this in the early days after Europe's liberation, or even right now today in certain hypernationalistic circles: "A man was lying on the brink of death; a Frenchman saw him and passed by. But a German . . . or a Russian, a Communist, a Negro, an Algerian, etc., was not afraid of showing kindness. He is the neighbor we must love—

[4] Lk. 10, 37.

he who acts charitably—whatever his race!" Very many Christians would be as doctors of the Law, Pharisees unable to grasp such a proposition. A blind, obvious hatred inspired by worldly interests or the fear of losing ill-gotten privileges, a powerful hatred able to contaminate whole peoples, races, or classes, casts its gloomy pall over vast collectivities whose individual members are often perfect models of virtue and charity. The Samaritans are all these neighbors detested and enshrouded by an unjust and cruel banishment. The curse is hurled: striking the innocent and the guilty, the decent little people as well as the cynical Nazis with their death camps.

In choosing the example of the Samaritan, our Lord teaches that they also are men, generous brothers and worthy of love as much as the Jews and more so than those mediocre, lax, selfish Jews. The love in their hearts draws men closer together and not the color of their skin any more than their blood or their dress or their dwelling places. Then we have freed ourselves from prideful chauvinism and Satanic jealousies in order to rise up to the nobleness of sentiment or good "sportsmanship" which will permit us sincerely to love everything good and noble in our greatest opponents!

No Mere Humanitarianism

However, our neighbor is not "everyone" in general. This parable is opposed to a vague humanitarianism. Philanthropy may lead us to a Platonic love of even the most remote peoples —who do not trouble us or get into our way. This double-dealing is not the evangelical spirit. And even if we are not indifferent to the lot of our fellow men in an otherwise shrinking world where peoples are brought into contact with each other through the advancement of communications, how much more ought the affairs of our neighbor interest us! Because most often our enemy is really our neighbor, who should be our friend. The worst fights are those found in a henhouse. Because today our planet is growing smaller and we are coming into closer contact with people, and because our means of communication, airplanes, rockets, radio, are only unfeeling mechanisms, threat of new wars breaking out ever increases. It is quite imperative that the telecommunications of charity be intensified to the extent of honing-down the infernal increase in friction among men. Everything which helps us to understand and love the good people of every country helps bring about peace on earth. The people of tomorrow will camp on our doorstep. There will no longer be people *out of contact* with each other!

Would we not be disillusioned if we terminated our exegesis here at this point? So far, even though it is difficult actually to carry out, even if it is eminently useful to this shrinking world of ours, we have not experienced any great spiritual uplift in this teaching. It is not, in fact, concerned with loving all men, but those who are good among men. We set aside those castes or deceptive categorizations that confuse the good with the bad. Ours is an equitable, intelligent, personal selection, for we cast the evil into hell and carry the good to heaven: that is to say, we hate the bad and love the good. Our neighbor—is good. But what is proper for the final judgment when the wicked are to be identified with evil, is not proper for our earthly state. "Love your enemies!"[5]

[5] Mt. 5, 44–48; Lk. 6, 27–36.

129

Christ's death tells us to love our real enemies—not only strangers —and it is a more wonderful, more mystical concept than the parable of the good Samaritan . . . at least such as it was understood by the doctor of the Law, and as we readily understand it. But is it too far-fetched to think of Christ smiling a bit ironically and thinking as he listens to the wise Jew's answer: "Now, let's see him try it out! Now, let him see men to be loved in the good Samaritans! It won't be so bad. . . ." To be more precise, he did not tell him: "I agree, I quite agree!", but simply: "Go and do likewise! Be like the Samaritan . . . and you will yourself be worthy of being loved." This very conclusion makes a false exegesis of this parable in sermons palatable. Let Christians so set at odds with each other, so often selfish, try to be as good as the anticlerical, as their enemies in general, and those who do good in particular, of course . . . and they will be worthy of love. They will be a pleasing neighbor to all. May God deliver the holy Church from the snares of certain religious, from certain bulldog priests! But these are only offensive attitudes! True evil lies in the heart and the Christian has no right to be selfish. His law is the Gift. If he gives himself, he will be loved and will help the Spirit of the Church to be loved. . . .

The Man of Sorrows

It appears as though our Lord must now become the means through whom we may surpass and develop the doctor's exegesis. We find much profit in identifying the man who comes down from Jerusalem to Jericho with the *passion of God made man*. This man, is he not God, descending from the heavenly Jerusalem and wandering the dangerous roads of earth along the Dead Sea—that corrosive stagnation of sin in which humanity is lost? By his incarnation God prostrates himself and exposes himself to the blows of criminals, his brothers. He goes out to the very rim of hell where Sodom and Gomorrah were swallowed up. From the kingdom of unity through love he committed himself to a world of division and hatred. From the infinite source of the Gift he was given this arid stretch of land where misery seeks full sway. He was given this region of terror which points the way to a floundering in the fetid mire of riches that people believed they possessed and which glue them and coat them, capture them and smother them in their deadly slime.

This man who comes to men is God become man, the Son of man. . . . This man who falls under the blows of robbers is Jesus in the hands of sinners—in our own dirtied hands which nail him upon the cross along the wayside, the way of his love. Why then do men seek to destroy God? Why do they wish to rob the one who gives himself? God is infinite power, infinite glory, infinite happiness—true happiness. He comes to bring man what he has and is. But we want to take it from him and not receive it because of our own blinding pride. Like so many Prometheuses we reach out a sacrilegious hand to the divine Fire. We mere creatures want God to give us godliness. We are so sensitive to the first and lasting temptation: "You will be like gods!"[6] Even while we snatch the crown from the hands offering it to us, he longs to crown us kings! He yearns to place the glory of supreme authority over our heads. But God is already illuminated with it and we can only profit from his liberality, we can only be debtors

6 Gen. 3, 5.

131

to him . . . and that is why we must kill God—so that we might be finally the First, with subservience to no one, especially no subjugation to love . . . for the acknowledgment of the heart is the most unendurable of servitudes. Consequently, men took hold of their King; they took advantage of the lowliness of his Goodness; they killed him; they are dead-set on killing him; and they never cease killing him. Every generation must take part in deicide, and every man must go to him with his whip and nails. As many men there are, that will be the number of God's enemies, God's assassins. They can never forgive him for being the First, for being humility, tenderness, and charity. They reject him as their brother. At best, they will admit of a God abstracted from its creation—a God who exists arrogantly and indifferently in its heaven, but this God made man can be only a false brother. God, as at Christmastime, was cast into a den of wolves: so much the worse for him! Men find weakness the most difficult thing to forgive. And therefore, in their name, Nietzsche scoffed at divine pity, despised the Lord's disciples who were "meek and humble of heart," contemptuously rejected this religion of "slaves" . . . and, in order to exalt his Superman, proclaimed the death of God!

Man without God

God is there, on the wayside, abandoned, bruised; seemingly dead. He intended us to be gods with him and through him by means of his grace. Men turned their backs on him, rejected this humbling gift; they preferred to be gods without God. Therefore they crucified him. As Creator he not only imposed his laws, but by his love, wanted to capture their freedom, to teach them to love obedience, to accept their bondage and lot in life, their position as creatures. To accept him as King. Relieved of God, they are free at last. And they have laid this God bare. Through their own intelligence, on earth, they give themselves their power, their glory, and their happiness. They have taken their own destiny into their hands; they have made their own laws and have selected their own goals. They create their civilization—by Man and for Man—this civilization where Man is alpha and omega, the beginning and the end!

Modern Babel, the apocalyptic fruit of its sins, is an imposing victory for man. Indeed, some will maintain that the transcendent God is not reached through any efforts of man. But this distant God means little to man. Sartre proudly states in *The Flies* that God's and Man's destinies sail parallel courses and neither intercepts or is aware of the existence of the other. Man wants to be his own God in Humanity. That God remains his God in his deity is what matters to him! This intervening God, this God who has created and who does not isolate himself from his work, this loving, faithful, and saving God is what Man does not want, refuses and kills. Man "without God" condemned Emmanuel (God with us). It is in his heart that man desires to kill and there he effectively succeeds in slaying his God. For it is there where he is vulnerable. Every man has the ability to kill God in his own heart and in the hearts of his neighbors. God puts himself at his mercy and the pride of the man does not know pity. He would be free from God's Love!

Temptation of God

We must repeat that there is no more insupportable servitude than that of love when we do not love. He who does not love, cannot hope to understand this affiliation any more than he can hope to understand fraternity. He views it as a cunning manoeuvre, a secretive inveigling. For love without defense, surrendered love (God was not beaten on the wayside: that is not said, neither was it done!), this love appealing to we know not what in a man whose pride does not admit it, this love which is considered an innate blemish, a weakness which is precisely the first corrupted gift of the creator. This love enkindles a response in the soul, a secret response, a "yes," an impulse that no imperious authoritarianism or logic can challenge. There is in man a son of God ready to revive and to hand over to his Father the key of the interior citadel. Such is the terrible temptation of God for the man in revolt. To wipe out every trace of God the man would have to kill his heart. Sovereign reason alone must triumph in him and in *his* society. Of course, we must not become pessimistic: today, God is not dead in all hearts. Yet, since the Revolution, man's independence has been officially proclaimed, and the states, including those whose members are Christians and believers, aspire not only to freedom from the churches, but from God as well. God has been officially and solemnly banished from the constitutions . . . and religious men no longer dare dispute against this fact. Certainly, God has no concern over liberty. We did not choose the ocean: but there it is and we must take it into our considerations. But we no longer wish to take

God into consideration. Officially, only the earthly paradise without God counts. The human race, cut off from its Creator, more and more impoverished without God, more and more meaningless, is easy prey to scientism and rationalism. It is mechanized, materialized, and moves constantly towards the functional anonymity of robots. It courts nothingness in a hell where love is abolished, the hopeless hell of concentration camps.

False Medicines and False Remedies

Among us God is dead. He is dead within us. . . . But his great corpse weighs heavily upon us. What must we do to revive it so that joy may once again ring out on earth? The sound and proper joy found in the beloved truth of our dependence on supreme love, this joy accorded by God which is only possible if God returns to life among us!

Can the priest, the Levite of the Law, do anything about it? The Law is powerless, and also powerless are religious formalism, the most symbolic ritualism, the most moralizing and the most dogmatic catechism. Neither will the solemn pomp of religious ceremonies, nor the most judicious liturgical reform, save Christ from death—and humanity with him. All that means nothing to a world shaken from the divine. It is comical or curious, coming from the remote past, or it is poetical, esthetical . . . at least a superstition discrediting man. We are not against a certain rejuvenation of cult; we rejoice over it, but we do not see it as a universal and infallible cure-all. This is only a relative aspect of the essential problem: how can we revive God in the souls of men? Fanatical and *exclusive* liturgical enthusiasm would only be a danger and a grave mistake. Ritualism, ineffective as it is in Latin or in any language, sees Christ dead and steps over his body. Sermons that fall upon their listeners like cold showers, icing their hearts, have no more power. Dogma is the basis of piety for the faithful so long as this dogma be not a science, a rational theology, compounded at will by the learned men of all ages, but that it be the living Truth of God, not only of the Law, that it be this personal God, this "living" God whom Pascal, fascinated and overcome, pressed to his heart: "God of Abraham, God of Isaac, God of Jacob! of philosophers and learned men."[7] The functionalism of the Levites, their devotion to the letter, to rubrics, to a ceremonial display as indispensable as changeable and secondary, the rigidity of professional priests, willing inquisitors out-doing the rules, organizations eager to place an infantile humanity under their supervision, the unchecked Law that encircles a closed religion—none of these whatever can do anything but leave Christ to die. Here we consider the Law in opposition to Charity. The Law is not evil if it receives its norms from Charity; but when it constitutes the very principles of religion, then it is a danger; it then becomes the agent of death! There are some priests and Levites who are grave-diggers of the first class. May their funereal ceremonies engulf them! Being unable to heal Christ on the wayside, it does not pay to hide him away; but they can still bury a half-dead man, stifling his cries, so they can escape from the problem he poses; they have it in their power to do away with him; they are capable of striking a legal blow

[7] "Memorial" found in Pascal's coat after his death.

right to his heart, making certain everything conforms to the rules, conforms to their "papers," to their "formulas." Let the stifling works of the legists in religion who make laws just to be making them, who smother the irrational beatitudes in their ratiocinations, the petty work of ritualists hiding the faith in the sanctuary and reducing it to mere punctilious displays—let these be the ancient liturgies the archeologists unearth and change with their inopportune discussions about particular paraliturgies. . . . They step over the dead Christ, victim of sin and not the law's failure, or the failure of dogma or ritual. Or they bury him beneath so many wrappings that were he not God there would be no hope for him!

They are secretly afraid of the truth of Christ. They prefer their religion for themselves, with its mechanics and its rationality. When love is linked to it, then to what folly of sacrifice will it not lead? They know not what the true life is which this God brings to man, which is infinite and can but gladden to the bursting point the souls of men who receive it.

They see Christ, suspect what he is—the interior revolution come to set the world on fire; their dry lips speak of it and coat the message, sclerose it with human wisdom and moral prudence, rendering it politically adaptable to this world. And when they understand it too well, they turn tail. If Christ's death ever moves them, if he ever calls them, what would he ask of them? They are of the opinion he would demand everything. No, they will give him nothing. Besides, what have they to offer? They got absolutely nothing . . . nothing but some books, nothing but science, the Gospel herbarium . . . of dead flowers.

The "Good" Samaritan

Only a loving heart can bring God to man. Love alone can conquer the death of God who was killed on earth by the conceited pride of mortals. God has endowed the hearts of his creatures with this wonderful power!

The heart—this is the Samaritan, the foreigner . . . no stranger to the God-man coming down from Jerusalem. The Samaritan is the son of God, brother of Christ, as is every man . . . but especially he, because he feels what moves the heart of the man-God. Divine love dwells in his man's heart. It is not alien to one whom it nourishes with its disinterested impulse at the risk of falling beneath the robbers' blows. But it is foreign to the priest of the Law, the Levite, and all they represent. The offices of priesthood and prophet, in the New Law, must merge into one; in the Old Law, before this synthesis took place, they were thesis and antithesis, the two dialectical elements of man's approach to God. A beneficial conflict! Today this conflict is harmful, so the Priest-Prophet is come among us to set up the new order of Charity. The ponderous weight of Judaism dampens Christian ardor, hinders the freedom of the children of God. The true mystery of charity has no worse enemy than the appalling incomprehension of the priests or Levites of the Law.

The heart is stranger and enemy to the intellect. The spiritual writers of the Middle Ages rightly distinguished between intellect and intelligence, between the exterior vision of beings who only consider appearances, reducing persons to the state of things, and the interior vision which sees into the real heart of beings and respects their freedom. Pure rationalism drains the blood of

men and transforms them into abstract mummies, heartless enti-
ties whose machinery of logic can only crush the reality of
humanity and God, the mystery of creation and the mystery of
the Creator. Between "this" intellect and the heart, in the Pas-
calian sense, there is no pity, only death. The intellect feeds upon
a terrifying hatred against every thought in which charity abides
—the same hatred that pitches Jew against Samaritan. The Jew
judged the Samaritan and considered him heretical. The Jew
passed judgment and condemned. The Christian does not judge
and pardon.

Coredemptive Man

Let us turn aside now from the priests and Levites of the Law—
these men who officially pretended to represent God—who have
caused so much harm in the Church because the Spirit of God
was not in them. Let us consider man's heart before the death
of the God crucified for him outside the gates of Jerusalem. It is
expressed with compassion. Love recognizes love and acts directly. It gives, it is given, it does not weigh and measure, and
it continues right up to the resurrection of God among men.
The parable of the good Samaritan beautifully teaches the co-
redemptive role of humanity—this humanity unsaved without
God, but which can be saved and divinized with God. The
supreme tenderness of divine charity cannot look upon any creature, even one enslaved by sin, without nobleness, and it does
not impose its grace and offers it with the blood and confers upon
him the dignity of saving God here below.

God is dead within all sinners; in them he awaits resurrection and every man is invited to take his part in this joyous miracle. At what price? How much will this cost? We have to seek the answer in St. Paul's praises of charity—this charity without which we are nothing, which is kind, patient, trusting . . . (1 Cor. 13). The Samaritan pours out oil and wine; he soothes and purifies the wound. Certainly, he does wrongly, for the absolute of truth and love makes no clever compromises with worldly wisdom. *Veritas liberabit vos.*[8] He pours a healing wine, a burning alcohol over the wound of error. He does not teach a glossed-over simplified religion. He grants no concessions, for he does not wish the *élite* to say: "So this is your religion—a formless, honeyed conglomeration!" He particularly does not want the Bread of Life to reproach him for having desired to make it "assimilable"! He uses a pure wine, a sacred bread, the absolute ideal which we never grasp that becomes the perfect star which the admiring soul cannot doubt, but only adore and love and follow from afar, sure of being guided to the crib, to divinization . . . for God will give men this star they hope for, to become gods in him and by him.

But he offers the real truth of salvation, insisting to us weak humans that sacrifice is necessary, that there is no flowering without a preliminary self-sacrifice, that everything comes from nothing—*todo y nada!*—, that the cross had to be endured before the glory of Easter. He declares, "Blessed are they who suffer! Blessed are the poor, the pure, the peacemakers, the persecuted!"; he says we must pardon our enemies and love them, and he insists that this is to preach the Gospel, and is not what it appears, a vicious blow, as one savagely would drive a nail into a

[8] Jn. 8, 32.

block of wood. We are not concerned, as the legists are, with crucifying the man. "My yoke is light," our Lord attests.[9] The cross is only heavy if we drag it. It carries, lifts up, and saves. But there still is suffering: the fear of God. How can the Absolute help but frighten mediocrity? How can the sinner not be afraid of holiness? The nocturnal owl flees from the sun. Moreover, the Samaritan took care to pour out the oil before the wine, though this is perhaps not recommended to those in charge of the sick. But kindness must prepare the way for truth. Charity is, like Christ, both human and divine. Without detracting from the Absolute which it radiates, it is reassuring, considerate, understanding, and tempered. *"Non potestis portare modo! You cannot bear them now,"* said Jesus.[10] Charity is uncompromising before evil; but if it acts gently towards the sinner, it also knows how to forgive, and in the act of pardon, beyond necessary sacrifices, it reveals the joy of divine truth.

All the saints know the strange antinomy of God's love which is as violent as the fire of holocausts and as soothing as the breeze which, for Elijah, blew on Mount Sinai. There is no raising of the soul to God without this gentle and devouring fire that salves and burns and paves the way to the bliss of the *unitas spiritus*.[11] Inspired by God, for God, for wounded humanity, the Samaritan, with force and gentleness, with a total love, but a love which does not destroy, which takes upon itself, raises up and transfigures, this kindly man, we say, comforts and prepares the ascent to

[9] Mt. 11, 30.
[10] Jn. 16, 12.
[11] This theme of the *unitas spiritus* is dear to spiritual writers. It designates the unitive way in its completion.

Jerusalem. God came down; he is left bruised and nailed to a cross; he awoke the love of men and only the Samaritan responded to God's immolation. Seeing that, man agrees to do something, and when he loves, salvation begins and the helpful Samaritan ascends with his God martyr. Apparently, it is man who helps God to ascend, who revives him and reopens heaven for him. In fact, it is the victim who helps his Saviour rise up. We live as egotists and all of a sudden the divine potential of generosity in us is confronted with some danger. We immediately forget our comforts; we out-do ourselves and we are the first surprised by it. As a result we ask ourselves just how we did respond to that extent. And it suffices that a new occasion arise and there we are summoned once again to surpass ourselves in charity!

Towards the Heavenly Jerusalem

Everything the Word of God says means something. Not for nothing was it said that the priest and Levite of the Law were coming down. They were descending into the corruption of Jericho, into the corruption of luxury and wealth, into base pleasures, the supreme humiliation of the proud, into the death from which no one can be revived—they were falling into what sticks to the spirit like cloying mud or befouling asphalt. They make a pretense at descending like God. It belongs to God alone to make himself incarnate: his love and might make it possible: God can enter the abjection of misery and grief, he can advance right into the darkness of the ignominious death among thieves. The muck in the grotto at Bethlehem is pure; the cross stream-

142

ing with blood is pure; the whole of creation is pure and even the horror, result of sin, is pure. Only what comes from the heart of the evil man is impure. But, to be identified with sin and not to be a sinner, we would have to be God, and the same is true for bearing the curse of sin without ever having committed it, and walking in our earthly slime without being splattered with it, in pulling us out of it without becoming soiled, without ripping the spouse's wedding garment.[12] The religion of men is intended to raise up; it is ascension to the Spirit—detachment and separation from the world. But this does not mean we have to abandon our bodies any more than the universe. The Christian looks to God; his religion is God—the Spirit; his purified spirit must raise itself up; and in raising itself it brings the body with it; with the body, he carries away the cosmos, just as with his soul, by fraternal charity, he leads humanity to which he is joined. He must not, at first, progress to his body or his brothers. He must desire the absolute Infinite who is his principle and his end. In giving himself to the Spirit he reëstablished the truth of his being. The disordered state was the submission of the soul to carnal passions, subjection to the world. The order places matter in its rightful place in a secondary position with the world alongside it—here we mean humanity saved or to be saved, considered from the point of view of faith; matter, in a secondary position, is not reduced to nothing, but it no longer blinds the soul; it is enlightened by it and the light which the soul communicates to it is the same as in God; the human community, a family which the Samaritan looks for and reconstitutes in the light of God, in the warm glow of divine Paternity, is not a servitude to vanities, a

[12] 2 Cor. 5, 21; Rom. 8, 3; Gal. 3, 13.

tangle of desires, it is really a community. Because one soul ascends to God, because it chooses God first of all, other souls and creation become crystallized around it. The higher the soul is lifted up, the mightier and more beautiful it becomes. The human brotherhood does not prepare for divine filiation. But it is because we love God that we become capable of loving men for eternity, not as a human convenience, but for heaven. They are only too much concerned with things of the earth; they alone seem to matter; they abandon themselves to outrageous evils until they turn about and slit their own throats! It would be ridiculous to believe that a world of conveniences and ultra-modern comfort would be better tolerated. Man's desires are like the Hydra's heads: when one is cut off, two new ones appear. . . . It would be the height of folly for anyone to believe that an equalitarian world—a human triumph—would be a touch-stone for the human race's turning to God. They constantly repeat: human brotherhood, then God; earthly happiness, then heaven; justice, then charity. But you do not climb up a staircase by going down it. We must first set up the order of values. Self-sacrifice is not the destruction of what is inferior to the spirit, but rather it is the putting of it in its proper place. God first of all because he is the First Principle . . . and nothing but God first, because in comparison to God all creation is as nothing. We have to begin with God just as they begin the study of arithmetic with the unit "one," and the sentence with a capital letter. First of all we must see God, see that men have killed him, lift ourselves up to bring him to life, approach him and with him ascend to Jerusalem. When God comes to life men will come to life and matter itself will be spiritualized. That is the problem, the only problem: God. Let us take hold of the needle and the thread will follow.

The Flesh and the Spirit

The heart ascends; Christ saved ascends, makes his ascension after his tragic incarnation: he ascends, sustained by the good Samaritan, carried by the good Samaritan's own mount. For the animal which carries this wonderful man is not neglected. He does not carry his donkey, but it carries him wherever he wishes to go, that is, on the way up to Jerusalem. What a journey this is, the journey of his life and an encounter with God at journey's end! This man draws near to the crucified God with his spirit leading his body and ruling over his senses. We could quibble over this point: it is not expressly mentioned that he ascends as it is said the others descended. But it is unimportant to say which it is: he is on his way to Golgotha and suffering, entering onto the path of sacrifice, and taking the redeeming sorrow of his God with him. With his arms outstretched and his heart receptive to God he chooses the narrow path leading from the cross into the fullness of heaven. This sole means to salvation is the way certain professors of spirituality are hardly in favor of today: for they flatter souls, make spiritual demagoguery and religious allowances. Deep in their hearts they reject suffering and sacrifice. They speak of Easter and brush aside Good Friday. But Paul answers them: "For I determined not to know anything among you, except Jesus Christ and him crucified ... *et hunc crucifixum!* (Christ crucified ... and no other)."[13]

The Samaritan leaps from his donkey and gives assistance to Christ; the mind renounces the flesh, mortifies and crucifies the flesh so that God may live in the world—and God already is alive in him. From that moment God is in the Samaritan's hands and,

[13] 1 Cor. 2, 2.

thus sustained, he mounts the donkey he rides. The mind placed God over the flesh. God is in him and pervades his entire being, and the remaining journey seems like a joyful triumph of a good man overjoyed in saving his God. But if God had not previously died the Samaritan would never have had the courage, the devotion, the persevering care. He must be on the look-out with God! We think we do all things and it is he who accomplishes everything. He becomes helpless in order to support us. We have seen in this mystery the loving freedom of that man being respected and satisfied: realizing its divine potential.

The finite love of a man multiplied by the infinite distress of God becomes the lever capable of lifting up the whole world and assuring God's resurrection in his creation. The parable of the good Samaritan shows us to what heights human generosity can reach—and the hero is certainly the one most astonished by it. He has the potential for the most unbelievable humility. He placed this dead God upon his beast and is entirely at his service. God takes his place in him, reigning in him: walking on foot alongside him, vigilant, attentive, and deferent: the crucified one is his king returning to his city, riding a donkey, and in fact Christ ascended into heaven with his body paving the way for the flesh sanctified by his agony and death.

The most delightful thing about this passage is not that the Samaritan becomes the slave of him whom he saves, but rather it is the extraordinary way he gives what he does not have. Indeed he gives what he has, but also what he will have. He pays the innkeeper two denarii. . . . "Take care of him; and whatever more you spend, I, on my way back, will repay you."[14]

[14] Lk. 10, 35.

146

In so doing he made God's protection his own concern, the concern of his life. He gives him all his past merits because before he actually encountered God on the wayside he was righteously on his way to meet him; he wasted nothing in the festivities at Jericho; he had a reserve of gold, not much really, but just the same, it was "his" money! No one doubts that he earned more from this encounter with Christ! Love knows neither limit nor measure. This fellow gives everything to his God—his past, his present, and his future: his life consecrated to the greatest service.

The Mercenary Innkeeper

Until then the whole story takes place between the Samaritan and his God. If we have mentioned other people, it was in reference to the robbers or the harbingers of the Law, those tinkling cymbals and sounding brass . . . it was in reference to the donkey and to the denial of the flesh—which has got to be accompanied by a renouncement of the world. But though both the flesh and the world are lost, they will again be found and transfigured. However, in the inn we find other people who take their part in the story: the employer, certainly also his wife, the maidservant and all the other menials. This place is as frequented as it is in ill-repute. The world does not lack more occupants than sinners. But on earth there are both death-traps and inns. What do we make of the innkeeper? "Take care of this man and whatever you spend beyond this for his care, I shall pay it when I return again." The Gospel immediately follows this with: "Which of these three, in your opinion, proved himself neighbor to him who fell among the robbers?" The innkeeper is really not involved for he is neither a sinner, a coward, nor a saviour. He takes in the divine victim and, we assume, takes proper care of him, but he is paid for his care, or at least, will be. He is not without some kind of merit, but he does it in the expectation of being rewarded by the Samaritan. He is a worthy mercenary: the hope of gain very wisely encourages him and becomes the very reason for his devotion—oh worldly wisdom! We shall doubtlessly have to deal with this kind of Christian who loves God to gain heaven, who performs his duties for love of the saints who have given all, who are sons of God. God lives among us middle-of-the-road Christians, profiteers of the divine, thanks to those who have spared nothing for God and have given him to us. Loving God for love itself, loving him for his goodness to us, is one stage of the spiritual life which is only a positive sign if directed towards generosity. If not, it may become one step further down on the way to betrayal: Judas betrayed in this manner for a few pieces of silver. But in the case at hand, seeing that the innkeeper does agree to an advance and decides to earn merit without being paid for his work right away, and seeing that he exhibits little of his immediate egotism and that he consents to some sacrifices on earth before "receiving" the joy of heaven, we may conclude that he belongs to that category of mediocre Christians with whom God gets along somehow, before the final judgment and the definitive return to Jerusalem, to Eternity! If God is entrusted to our care, if God is among us, however precariously and wretchedly, we owe it to the holiness of good Samaritans. All is not without God on earth; there is still the poor inn of worthy men who are not very worthy in love. . . .

The Climax of Charity

Why did the good Samaritan fade out of the picture? We do not witness his return to the inn. We are only left to imagine that he abandoned the God-man, Emmanuel, without thinking of death. As for us, we prefer to believe that in giving the two denarii, he gave his whole life; he gave himself "body and soul" to the mercenary so that he might take care of God and do God's work here below. He devotes himself to poor mankind—entirely—for God so that he might live among us and not be driven out of us right away. For the benefit of mankind, which is the same thing as for the glory of God. The good Samaritan gives his life and by his death earns what yet remains to be earned so that men will not separate themselves from this God who is born again on earth. When the good Samaritan returns, it will be the hour of this innkeeper's death and that of his wife, maids, and servants . . . it will be the hour of this mediocre humanity's death which will follow God triumphantly to remain with him in the heavenly inn—the welcoming inn where love is the only money. And this will come to pass thanks to the sacrifice of the good Samaritan who so well imitates the God of love that we are easily led to confuse him with his Master, Jesus Christ. The encounter on the way of the cross has transformed this kindly man into another Christ. "It is now no longer I that live, but Christ lives in me," wrote St. Paul. . . .[15] We become like God at the paroxysm of charity.

Our neighbor—the good Samaritan—is therefore he who loves God—God in his love for mankind, for God alone is his love—

[15] Gal. 2, 20.

and he it is who keeps this God of love among men, who pays for his stay with the merits of his life and even his death. If the Samaritan gives us God, it is chiefly because he loves God, but it is also because he loves men. In understanding that God died for men in order to be with them, he begins to love his brothers as God and he sacrificed everything to help his God realize his plans for humanity. Such is the power of a great love. Nothing is closer to us than the Samaritan who brings us nearer to God, who gives God to us; it is truly fitting that we love him as much as ourselves, more than ourselves, more than anything. God is always more Father than brother. His divinity merges into his humanity and his brotherhood takes on a transcendent character. For his dedication the good Samaritan received the true spirit of brotherhood from Emmanuel—a spiritual brotherhood that aids us in loving at first the souls of men. Joined to God, they will love themselves more and will not fight for the bones of earthly happiness and justice will come more easily, as will peace and joy. It is disturbing how often even our Christian sociologists look at the problem from the wrong angle. The apostle, the saint, is the true brother of every man, who pays dearly for his brotherhood and sometimes with the extreme of martyrdom. It is not enough to love him as a brother, but as another self. As a matter of fact, loving him as a brother would be to love him as yourself . . . but we are accustomed to consider "our brothers" as "others," not our neighbor certainly, and indeed not our enemy, but a stranger. Our brother is of the same stock as ourselves, but he leads a parallel life pleasantly near, pleasantly indifferent, a similar life and yet a different life. It is this "otherness" which our

Lord forbids. Love unites. If we return a little of his love to the Samaritan he will in a certain sense enter into our intimacy. He has loved us and has offered his life and death for us. He is bound up in our existence and we have not got the right to separate him from us with a Platonic mentality. Love evokes love . . . and the characteristic of true love is that it changes the center of our life. He who loves his neighbor no longer makes himself the term of his spiritual quickening; the other becomes the end where his ego is utterly deflated and entirely offered. The Samaritan is lost in us and we lose ourselves in him; we find ourselves again "Samaritans" and he discovers himself as "us." This communion in which each makes the other the object of his love through a wonderful exchange is only possible through the Christ who lived in the Samaritan whom he has given us. God made man is the intersecting point of all human loves—the center of human brotherhood. The crossroads of the cross has become the inn of this charity which is love of God and neighbor.

We see that this parable is one of the more prominent. It reveals that love is a gift, that God has not failed in love and that his sacrifice excites the deepest love—divine love—among men. We are far from the Law. Our neighbor practices charity (*agapē*); we must love him, that is, imitate him to the point of becoming others ourselves, other good Samaritans.

Look about you. There are unfortunate people. It is fitting that we assist them and dress their wounds. But this is only a small sore upon humanity. The great shame which must be seen, which must not be overlooked, even under the pretext of broth and togs, is the death of God, this pit of despair which hollows out the heart of mankind. The bodies of God decay as much as our brothers'; that is the great plague. The death of God—the great evil, and that alone.

Perhaps we think we draw nearer to our brothers by means of charity and social reform; but we have not understood their essential misery—this God dead within them, wretchedly dead. We did not sense this infinite misfortune because we were distant from our brothers, spiritually quite distant as though in another world. Let our eye be less discerning, our soul more sincere, our mind truer, and then we shall perceive and understand why the world is in agony. With the help of grace we shall bring the dead God to life and we shall again live with our brothers in the paschal mystery of his Presence.

The Lost Sheep

THIS parable profoundly stirs up Christian feelings. In the early days of the Church the image of a shepherd carrying a sheep across his shoulders was more familiar to Christians than the cross is to us, the cross upon which hangs the Lamb of God cursed, abandoned, and with no shoulder to support him but only the rough crossbeam onto which his hands are nailed. These two images constitute the unsurpassed diptych of mercy's triumph over justice. The shepherd became one of us, an innocent lamb among the lost sheep, and he died upon the gibbet in order that the extraordinary parable of the lost sheep might be fulfilled and mercy might be taught abruptly to a sinning humanity.

Indeed our legists, our Pharisees, have so knowingly pointed out the stupidity of this shepherd who leaves ninety-nine sheep exposed to the likely attack of robbers and savage beasts just to save one foolish, presumptuous, and selfish sheep. It is insulting to the whole company of the faithful that the joy of heaven should be greater over the return of one prodigal soul than for all the rest, and all the more so because we now find ourselves here in the midst of an assembly of the faithful jealous like the elder brother and enraged because his father ordered the fatted calf slain! They are good and patient sheep, hardly ever thought about, only noticed if they should chance to run off. Should we be led by the logic of their ill-considered lessons, such parables would quite discredit God.

The Good Shepherd and the Unfaithful

Yet Christ seems to be teaching something here which goes without saying. "What man of you having a hundred sheep, and losing one of them, does not leave the ninety-nine in the desert and go after that which is lost, until he finds it?" This is only the normal procedure if we speak of souls under the law of charity. Ezekiel[1] foretold the Messiah would be the Good Shepherd and we see Christ declaring himself the door-keeper, and even the doorway itself, welcoming the flock.[2] The sheep hear his voice; he calls them—each by name;[3] he is no stranger to them, but their beloved leader whom they follow, who finds them food and who watches out for their safety, leads them into the peace of his kingdom and even lays down his life for them so that harm—whatever it may be—will not snatch those entrusted to him who are already in the flock, and the others who have yet to be united to the flock so that there may be but one flock and one shepherd. "I am the good shepherd, and I know

[1] Ez. 34, 11–31.
[2] Jn. 10, 7.
[3] Jn. 10, 3.

mine and mine know me, even as the Father knows me and I know the Father."[4] The knowledge of the heart leading to the extreme of complete sacrifice for others valued as much as himself, more than himself, takes for granted the same bonds between the sheep and Christ as there are between the Father and Son. They are, then, children of God and eternal love abounds in them through Christ. Therefore, we cannot tolerate the equity of the Law which demands tooth for tooth in the world of the sheep, but we must live rather the law of sacrifice, the law of giving! Souls are to be saved: this is the goal and nothing must be spared to that end. Every calculating mercenary is excluded from this divine family where love is indispensable at the foot of the cross.

Therefore it is normal for the shepherd to look for the lost sheep, that soul in danger of death. Who among you would not do so? This is required of all Christ's disciples. This poses no obstacle to the apostles and all who live according to the law of charity . . . no more than it is a difficulty to parents whose children have come to ruin: they will not rest peacefully until they are set back again on the right path.

Destiny of the Faithful Sheep

If it is in accord with our hearts to search out the lost sheep among the brambles and rocks, if we admit that the salvation of one soul is worth any sacrifice, worth even our lives, is it nonetheless a wise thing to risk failure and expose the safe ones to danger and compromise the salvation of the faithful? This is the

[4] Jn. 10, 14–15.

"foolish" divine wisdom. Think what we will, it is obvious that on the level of the story when it is a question of sheep in flesh, blood, and wool, it is unwise to leave the flock unprotected in the desert even if this desert (the *midbâr*) is plainly an untilled waste-land, though with sufficient grass particularly after the winter rains. To please the "knowing ones," let us say that the good shepherd, leaving them as he does in green pastures with sufficient food, does not entirely abandon the just.

But for our part we think charity is always the winner on the spiritual scoreboards. If ours were the exegetical conception of a monk of the Middle Ages, we would perhaps say we have got to renounce all our goods, even the legitimate, symbolized by the faithful sheep, for the sake of the one essential thing which is the salvation of our soul. But we, preferring to be objective, state that the paradoxical law "He who loses his life will find it"[5] is not only applicable to our personal life, but to the apostolic life as well. We find in this law a condemnation of the conservative mentality which crippled the Church in its expansion. We see again the worthy bishop anxious for his diocese and mission lands. The clergy of the diocese are found diminished in numbers . . . as though the Holy Spirit depended on the cares of the episcopal administration, depended on the distribution of priests to their traditional posts!

If, on the other hand, priests are found overburdened with devout parishioners to the extent that they are left with neither the time nor the energy to carry the message of love to those still in darkness, then we may say that their parish—although bustling with activity—is sclerosed and near death. It is a question of

[5] Mt. 10, 39; 16, 25.

those who know how to say "no" to all that the Christian people and clergy draw from human wisdom, from the importance the canons gave to superstition in spiritual matters to political cleverness with the temporal power, continuing to a reverential reference to the psychology of crowds and individuals.

Let them make excuses for our insisting on these renowned ninety-nine sheep. Someone has written, "We must not concern ourselves over the sheep mentioned in the parables: they are only used for contrast!"[6] It is as if he were saying the sheep are but paper cut-outs like we made in grade school art classes. No! We shall not abandon the faithful sheep like this, even if the shepherd seems to have forsaken them, whereas in reality he saves the just in saving the lost. By offering them a joyful return to the fold he removes their temptation to take flight! He gives them another yearning instead to do as he. Here is my shepherd who, only mindful of the guilty, rescues him at the peril of his life; faithful souls directly take into account the value of one soul. What is to be done? They do not want to be separated from their pastor (he left them, not abandoned them); they are electrified by the love animating him and they leave their false security to follow the master in pursuit of sinful souls; and they are in the same danger with him, prepared to lay down their lives for lost souls. The flock is engaged in the great battle of redemption. This is truly a flock of the just! In the same way a good parish is only justified in God's eye if it suffers and sacrifices for those who are not yet protected under the Saviour's crook. This, of course, takes for granted that each Christian soul is filled with love of neighbor!

[6] Denis Buzy, *Les Paraboles,* Beauchesne, 1932, p. 139.

Unity of the Flock

We note here that we are speaking of a flock, that is, of something communitarian. By as much as this parable is deeply linked to the *good Samaritan,* so it is to the *lost drachma* and the first half of the *prodigal son.* But the golden drachma bearing the king's effigy typifies the similarity between the soul and God, a resemblance that sin obliterates, and which is only found again thanks to this woman who is the Church, who sweeps and cleans, thanks to the light of the Holy Spirit—Love and Truth.[7] The prodigal son recalls how intimate is the bond uniting the soul to the Creator—this soul which the folly of false freedom locks outside the divine milieu.[8] The flock of sheep illustrates the humble cohesiveness of the members of the Mystical Body who enter into good pasture lands without any one of them superseding the other. The absence of a single member places the whole organism in jeopardy. That is the chief reason why the shepherd's devotion to the lost sheep is really the salvation of the weakened and exposed flock just now beginning to scatter. For as long as the lost sheep is kept away from its rightful place in the flock, the flock becomes one to be saved. For the just must also be saved. Their salvation is not inborn, not a certain fact. They are lost with the lost one, responsible for its wandering away; they did not know how to keep it with them; their jeopardized fidelity needs pardon and grace to strengthen and find again its perfection with the return about to fill them with joy,

[7] Lk. 15, 8–10.
[8] Lk. 15, 11–32.

united in the joy of the Saviour and his "friends," the saints in heaven responsible one for the other, hurt by a fall, exalted by a redemption![9]

Therefore, as the Lord declares: "Who would not do it?" they contribute to the salvation of the faithless. If they safeguard unity among themselves and guarantee salvation for themselves and their neighbor who must be found and reinstated in the group, the faithful cannot be shocked at their Master's words: "Rejoice with me, because I have found my sheep that was lost."[10] The fact is he carries the lost sheep on his shoulders and we do not desire to argue over whether it is there because it was wounded—as though it were not sufficient to have been lost, as though humanly he could do nothing else, or as though lawfully it was damned by mortal sins and spiritually dead! But now that it is on his shoulders as a result of the Saviour's strength and not by its own, it is revived and truly renewed. Christ's pardon is total, leaving nothing of sin and enmity. Friendship is there, born again, and the Lord has done this. He is happy because it cost him something, and what it cost concerns him alone. It is not easy to give one's life . . . but it is a joy for one who loves. The mercenary is incapable of this. Lacking this folly, he betrays. The sheep who forsake the shepherd and the lost sheep are scattered and go to their perdition. They betray. Fidelity is following Christ everywhere and testing to the point of death itself this basic precept: love others as yourself.

"I say to you that, even so, there will be joy in heaven over

[9] Lk. 15, 6.
[10] Lk. 15, 6.

one sinner who repents, more than over ninety-nine just who have no need of repentance."[11] Christ is explicit; he states this disturbing equation in which unity is worth more than the ninety-nine others. From this we conclude that the just man converted is worth more than the just who dwell in holiness and have no need of the good Shepherd's heroic intervention. We think this interpretation is not quite exact. We ought to say that no one is just and that everyone needs conversion, that all are beneficiaries of grace earned by the redeeming sacrifice. Thus, everyone has right to heaven's rejoicing over his salvation! We should also say that here Christ emphasizes the role of the sinner: he repents; he cooperates with grace; he forsakes his stolen freedom and is left to be taken, carried by God; he recognizes his dependence on God's love and strength; his attitude is without conceit. For it he had to change his life and renounce the evasive pleasures of the world; for it was not written that the lost sheep was found in the brambles. The sheep had to heave his flock for tempting grasses. It wallowed in happiness directed towards itself alone; the shepherd's love was the stronger. Before the wolf, the robber, have a chance to surprise it with a sudden unrepenting death, the mighty and gentle hand of the Master recovers it and it agrees to return again into the community of the flock. Psychologically, there is sometimes greater merit and indication of a more intensive love in this than in unflagging loyalty. To be sure, they who turn again to love are the more tempted, more sinful, but also the more generous creatures. Are not people like Charles de Foucauld more admirable, in compliance with St. Paul, than many Christians habituated as they are to little sins

[11] Lk. 15, 7.

and a mediocre faith? Finally, since the faithful sheep are actually virtuous Christians, we can at least imagine they shared in the Saviour's boundless joy. We may assume they took part in the rescue, praying for this intention, fervent and eager to set out on the adventure: the salvation of the sinner is their concern as well! Their friend the lost sheep finally takes its place in their benevolent flock!

The Fullness of Joy

While suggesting these admissible explanations, we would like to offer this one we are partial to. A greater *joy* does not necessarily mean the converted sheep is of greater value. But what is joy unless we are fully receptive to it, when everything is in order, complete? As long as our stomachs remain empty, we are ill at ease, and this is not bliss! As long as there is an unsatisfied desire in our senses or intellect or in our heart, the fullness of pleasure is impossible. . . . In the same way, a tiny spot is quite enough to disfigure a white page, and before our eyes and the interior feeling connected with it can be set at ease, the disturbing spot has got to be cleaned off. Now in our case, the spot represents the sinner. He has slipped away from the Christian collectivity. This collectivity is disturbed about it and cannot attain happiness; the story mentions only one lost soul; but it is like a toothache which distresses the whole body. We observed that this parable, through the image of the flock, contains, in comparison with the others, a communitarian aspect. Ours is a parable of the Mystical Body. It teaches this wonderful truth: in the tremendous spiritual family, perfect joy is only attained when all

161

the members are gathered together so as to be one flock with one shepherd. Then, around this flock, all the other creatures of heaven are gathered. This will be the glory of the end of the world, the eternal unblemished joy, a joy like the sun in a cloudless sky, this joy made possible only to the leader, Christ, to the Christians, his flock, to the angels, his friends, when redemption is fully accomplished. As long as there is a soul in peril, as long as a soul is yet to be saved, there is sorrow in the Mystical Body and redemption is incomplete; no one can collect his thoughts to experience his joy; everything is arranged so that the family exists and exists in its totality and in its absolute truth. There is so great a joy for the return of one soul, because then joy is made possible to all!

The Exemplary Unjust Steward

LUKE 16, 1–13

Yes, this steward, whose usual epithet—alone—implies censure, is commendable. The Gospel expresses it quite well: "And the master commended the unjust steward, in that he had acted prudently,"[1] for some people look upon prudence as a cunning grafting. They forget that prudence is the temperer of virtues, the "regulator" which directs men in the concrete circumstances of their lives and is not content with theoretical affirmations that prefer good as opposed to evil, but it is responsible for doing good and avoiding evil, and it is that which permits us to keep effectively on the right course even in fog or darkness. Furthermore, in the following sentence our Lord uses the word "wisdom" . . . for wisdom is also something concrete: it savors[2] the food before chewing it; it allows us to reject what is bad and to savor what is good. And so, wisdom gives prudence the additional impetus of goodness, the joy of work, the joy when we take the time to

[1] Lk. 16, 8.
[2] Wisdom, from *sapientia*, derived from *sapere*, to savor.

appreciate. Prudence steers a difficult course and has little time to enjoy the leisure of goodness. Therefore, we say again with Christ—and may he who judges otherwise be reprimanded—long live the prudence of the unjust steward! It is to be followed. But beware the unfaithful steward: he is an unsafe man courting disaster. Nothing is worth the infidelity of insuring one's future. And if we speak of improvident virtue, why not praise the virtue of unfaithfulness?

Of course, remarks such as these would be enough to make our eyes dart out of their sockets, but the motive of the "faithful one" restores the situation! It introduces into this Gospel account a supple exegesis worthy of the first prize in gymnastics, worthy of the man-serpent. *In petto,* the exegete works himself into a sweat as he protests against the Church for keeping this scandalous parable in the liturgy of the Eighth Sunday after Pentecost so long after it awkwardly placed it there.

Personally, we admit to being the nonplused preacher we now enjoy making sport of. We were that preacher until one day we noticed the idea of goodness crept up again and again in our commentary. There were a hundred crystals of goodness in our homily . . . these crystals danced before our eyes. Everything seemed to crystallize into one tremendous precious stone, into the purest of water. This rather disturbing and questionable parable became for us the sublime parable of goodness.

A Perplexed Exegesis

Until then, "as everyone," we were dead-set on defending the holy Scriptures against every ill-willed interpretation: "No, that does not mean we have the right to steal, unless it be in the case of necessity, and then only with certain qualifications. No, it doesn't mean that fools have no right to misuse a confidence—because inevitably it will all go wrong, but it means that the cunning man has all the privileges and merits, and in addition, the admiration and praise of those whom he has duped."

Certainly, when we read the sacred text we should not refrain from admitting that the master does admire and does commend the cautious thief. We should well recognize in the depths of our heart that one does follow the affair with interest; it is repugnant and deceptive. The steward is a lazy man or a profligate. "He has squandered the goods" of the rich man who employed him. When the employer at least uncovers his fraudulent actions, he calls the guilty one to him and demands he give account. We find nothing surprising in that. Then the steward says to himself, "What shall I do, seeing that my master is taking away the stewardship from me? To dig I am not able; to beg I am ashamed. [He has never done anything and is not at all decided upon changing his life to make it finally a worthy life of toil of any kind.] I know what I shall do, that when I am removed from my stewardship they may receive me into their houses [it does not take him long to reach the outrageous solution—and how efficacious it is]." "And he summoned each of his master's debtors and said to the first, 'How much do you owe my master?' And he said, 'A hundred jars of oil.' He said to him, 'Take your bill and sit down at once and write fifty.' Then he said to another, 'How much do you owe?' He said, 'A hundred kors of wheat.' He said to him, 'Take your bill and write eighty.' "[3]

[3] Lk. 16, 3–8.

Nothing could be more dishonest. The master learned of it and he who before the steward's squandering had harshly demanded an accounting and had decided to fire him purely and simply now—and this is bewildering—congratulated the steward for his dishonesty. It is no more a question of clearing up the affair. The rich man slaps him on the shoulder and says "Bravo!" The unjust steward triumphs at the very height of his disloyalty.

The disturbed moralists—and how can we not excuse them!— look to save the divine message in order to render this Bread of Life more palatable. It is a question, certainly, for Christian moralists. For the rest the case is settled: there again is more proof of the depravity of the Christian religion. Ah! If this page were not to be read at Mass, how many respectable ecclesiastics would take pleasure in skipping it altogether and allow it to sink into a pious and profound oblivion! But constrained to preach it, they dash headlong into the following lines of this amazing parable: "for the children of this world, in relation to their own generation, are more prudent than the children of the light. And I say to you, make friends for yourselves with the mammon of wickedness, so that when you fail they may receive you into the everlasting dwellings." Whew! Fortunately, heaven crops up here (the tabernacles or everlasting dwellings). The mention of heaven reassures and gives the whole parable an "honest purpose." The parable indeed teaches an excellent means of attaining paradise. . . . By dint of reflection they confess that the wicked cause themselves a lot of trouble to gain their ends, more so than the children of the "children of the light"! Of course, the children of the light are at a disadvantage, for they cannot sanction these methods . . . but they are too often conservative, grown dull in their virtue without dreaming of the social dangers. They let the darkness fill in all around them and discover themselves helpless and alone in the night, unable to hear each other's voice. Their case is lost unless a miracle from above saves their compromised situation. They conclude from this: "Let us be brave men, by all means. . . . But let it not prevent us from seeing things in their true perspective, from being active, modern, committed. Let us get organized, collect our material, coordinate our efforts! Let us profit from the circumstances; let's get to work! Let's be up to date—in line with progress—and even beyond that!" Thoughts like these are advantageous to us, for Christians everywhere, in the sciences, the press, the movies, television, not to mention syndicates and politics. We must fight for the kingdom of heaven, and if not, the poor . . . !

In spite of this exegesis we cannot help feeling remote from the parable and the praising of the unjust steward: the example is quite poor and misleading, though the lesson is excellent. We shall be discerning apostles, we shall form a strong Catholic action. Very well! But what will result, we wonder, from this proposition, this unparalleled order where the end justifies the means: "Make friends for yourselves with the mammon of wickedness!"?[4] We are always brought back to this shameless predicament of the dishonest steward, and of course, to the rich man's felicitations—not God's, evidently! Yet in spite of these barefaced congratulations, the traditional exegesis makes the rich man a type of God. And the steward is mankind—us.

[4] Lk. 16, 9.

Justifying Almsgiving

Our overworked minds hit upon a new solution. Charity, in the sense of giving relief to the poor, almsgiving. And this leads us to social and economic considerations. This parable seems disturbing for a good reason: our miserable earthly state where the absolute cannot be realized, where the saint cannot live in a pure state, because everything is relative and the good man is linked to sinning humanity. How can you step into mud without being soiled? Unfortunately, we are compromised. How can we get out of it? How, just the same, despite everything, despite the inevitable stain of the world upon those living in the world, can they be saved? Plainly, by generosity . . .

The rich man is God who has created all things and who has given man his earthly goods. Now, as a result of original sin, these goods from which we cannot escape are soiled and in turn soil. Now, theoretically, we are but lease-holders because these goods are only lent to us. But normal psychology decrees that we may use them as our very own, only for ourselves, with no consideration of God, in mercantile harmony with our neighbor (the latter being codified by history and laws, regulated by justice). Now, human justice is not divine justice. The most explosive commentators go almost to the point of declaring that ownership is thievery; others are content with saying money is mammon . . . the mammon of wickedness. And even if we have never been unjust in our business dealings, the fact alone of having money is a pact drawn up with mammon. This money has gone through so many dirty hands that it is soiled beyond repair. Besides, Christ declared: God or mammon![5] We must choose between him and money. We must become poor. That is the ideal, the impossible ideal our Lord desired to correct by the audacious parable of the unjust steward. The poor themselves need money, a little money, and it suffices, all things considered, for the spirit of poverty. Nevertheless, he who has this outlook possesses always an unjust money and goods over which he does not have rightful ownership either before God or man. All the same, what is he going to do to save himself—to get out of this dilemma of God or money? He will help himself to this accursed money with the intention of making it productive of good. Whether he has stolen or has the profit of stolen goods, he is left with this possibility from heaven: generous almsgiving . . . Besides, this parable is quite astute and may permit, according to the homily, certain lucrative adventures. The men who feel themselves at fault and who all the same desire to play both games to win heaven are able and worldly men who know quite well how to be charitable: they will get it all back in heaven. Having profited from their earthly existence, they will be found welcoming the eminent assembly of "their" poor into heaven. Alas, the worthy men of easy conscience are not always so generous. They lack cunning, for they also use the goods of earth with a false good conscience; they are compromised also and must not justify themselves with the excuse of having never filled their pockets at someone else's expense. They also must for their salvation become friends of iniquity by their sacrifices. Almsgiving alone lets them live in peace, putting them at rest in the

[5] Mt. 6, 24.

world of mammon. It is the great counterbalance, the counterbalance of evil . . . and almost pardon at the same time as it is sin. Evidently, preachers do not arrive at such conclusions; but the poor sinners craving heaven easily turn to this line of thought that is being offered them as they listen to commentaries on the unjust steward. Let us be monopolizers of God's goods. Let us use them to our advantage. Let us waste . . . but we know how to compensate our vices by this virtue that "covers a multitude of sins," by this goodness which wins our neighbor's heart and therefore the heart of God. And so we shall be like unjust stewards and, despite everything, despite that, by our liberality, we shall have the right to the eternal congratulations of the indulgent Lord.

This bargaining, this Simon-like swapping of spiritual happiness for a few acts of charity or even large donations, has something both hateful and childish about it at the same time . . . and God doubtlessly takes pity on those who practice it and takes into consideration a real humility of too little guilt, too entangled, and considers it a desire for a better world and an overt tenderness to one's neighbor. After all, it is better to give out a little of what one has in one's hand than to keep it all for oneself! The very fact of giving supposes that one is not completely hardened and not totally possessed by mammon. . . .

Spiritual Exegesis

Actually, we are quite far removed from a genuine religion, far removed from our parable. Christ, certainly, if he wishes to be merciful to our imperiled unfortunate ones, can teach them. From what we have said, the idea of goodness remains, but it is a spiritual goodness. It is the most marvelous kind of goodness for it is this which not only gives but also forgives. Here we have a parable analogous to the king's debtor.

To discover the meaning of a parable we must transpose it from the temporal plane to the spiritual. It may be that the story on the temporal plane is disconcerting and manifestly scandalous —just as the prophet Joel's behavior. In the same way a tapestry is odd-looking wrong side up and splendidly meaningful right side up. When our Lord speaks of the sower, he does not intend to teach us how to sow; if he speaks of hiring, he does not mean to recommend the vine-dresser's method of summoning laborers at every hour any more than he desires to give accountants a system for paying workers. We must proceed resolutely towards the mystical plane. Our parable is not concerned with teaching how to use temporal goods spiritually. These goods as well must be transformed to the spiritual plane by the magic wand of anagogy. They are spiritual goods.

This, then, is what our understanding, above and beyond reason, must "read" into the story of the unjust steward whom the master praised. The master is God; rich in goods. He has filled the souls of men with the wealth of his love, purity, and holiness; he has filled them with his grace. All the powers of the spirit—and what depend on the spirit—are the treasures which man manages usually quite badly, which he shamefully dissipates. Sin impoverishes the soul which ought to bear fruit and shine with merits. Every man filled with love must respond by love; and this is what Richard of St. Victor calls "love due." Unmotivated love is not like God, grace given in profusion, the principle of every gift. If by sin man loses, squanders, or kills the grace within him, he is incapable of responding to God and of rendering him what is due: he is in debt, and if the debts are too great, it is possible that God will cease communicating his wealth, will stop giving his grace. The sinner then perceives himself deprived of every good, of every possibility of doing some good and even the possibility of loving God. This is damnation. . . .

However, punishment does not immediately press upon him. The menace is there and the sinner is given advanced warning in the form of a final grace. He knows that he will suffer a severe judgment if he does not do something. What? He thinks about it and he is right in doing so; he is prudent. The sinner must have this prudence of thinking about his death and judgment, particularly his spiritual death which can precede death; for he must fear the grace which passes never to return! He then must be praised for this first bit of prudence which is a conscious hold upon the reality of his spiritual state and the destiny which awaits his negligent and disordered soul. As we are all sinner to some degree or other we have got to have the wisdom of seeing where we are as sinners and of thinking about how we must attempt to remedy a situation which is perhaps graver than we imagine because of the rut or slovenliness we are in.

"What shall I do? Without God I am nothing. All the same I cannot work the earth! I am made for higher things; I cannot allow myself to live by complete materialism!" We are not disparaging farming. The earth is used in this case in opposition to heaven, or more exactly, to all divine values on the order of grace. The sinner who has squandered so much wealth from above benefits from another source as his body, as the world. He looks for a way to avoid falling to the level of worldly desires and practices to which he may become addicted through their base desires. In short, this sinner has not renounced his ideal.

"To beg I am ashamed!", he adds. Work, in fact, is at the bottom of the action; it manifests the freedom and power of an individual and allows him to achieve or keep a certain autonomy. Begging, on the contrary, is the acknowledgment of a great downfall, of a resignation of his ego. Is the sinner devoid of God going to solicit grace from men? When God fills a heart, he frees it. But men most often bind and subject. That is all the more the case here since begging cannot support spiritual goods, for the soul which loves according to God is capable of radiating the gifts of God which save them from the chains of evil. The vagrancy of the beggars must not deceive us: it is an instant slavery reaping incessant rejections: the beggar is not even good enough to serve; from bondage to bondage he goes on his way to death . . . a rag left along the wayside is he. The unjust steward does not want to be one of these beggars, these play-things of the idols of the world, the toy of their passions. No one, if he is not of God, can give him the true richness which lasts, which is worthy, which makes the man, if not a supreme authority or the owner, at least a manager, an authority who wears his badge of office. He would blush at such a lowering of himself: the mighty or the rich of this world are turned so easily into broken puppets at the mercy of their senses, their interests, and their vanities—lords over all the earth perhaps are they, but possessed by the earth, hollow and empty in the despair of heaven, of men and of themselves. There would be much to

173

say on the last end of these "great men." They are without God; already they are forgotten by men; in the implacable truth of their empty existence, having gleaned everywhere, except from the Father, they despise themselves. The cautious sinner, enlightened by fear which is the beginning of wisdom, does not want to go the way of the prodigal son begging the food of pigs—hollow husks.

The Work of Pardon

He declares: "I know what I shall do. . . ." He has found the great means of salvation which God reserves to sinners. He is going to summon each of his master's debtors who find themselves in his power, who have received from God and have not responded by their merits, the normal and owed fruition of the love accorded them. He does not summon them in order to overwhelm them or to demand that they pay off their debts to the master. He does not become overzealous after the manner of the Pharisees. He is not going to be like the man who could not see the beam in his eye, but only the mote in his brother's—he will not tell the master: "I am not perfect, I admit it, but I am better than this man! Punish him and spare me." Neither will he say: "Admire the zeal which is consuming me. I have not given you much from what you have given me. . . . But see how the others, thanks to me, are finally paying their debts." He knows it is not enough to be an apostle, that he must be a saint; besides, the true saint alone is an apostle and leads his neighbor to give back to God love for love. Each man's destiny is a personal affair, not in the sense that he must be cut off from his neighbor, but in the sense that no one will save us in our behalf, that no one can pay our debts for us. We must at least lend a hand. Fellowship can only come about if it finds a freedom which welcomes and utilizes it.

The sinner knows he is a sinner and does not try to hide it; he does not play-act devotion in order to accomplish in others what he has not got. As for giving them something, it is impossible. He envisaged himself a beggar: well, he has lost the treasure of God, he did not share in it—and that is why he is so harshly reproached. Spiritually impoverished, he cannot, as the saints, let sinners in debt "share" in his merits, that help so vitally necessary to bring back the state of grace . . .

What is he going to do? He is a steward. Others depend as he on the master, but he occupies a privileged position, a place of responsibility, not for his actions alone: he manages others. This is not an essential aspect of the parable. Nevertheless, it has its own value. The steward is not simply every man with his particular grace to spread about, every man in relation to himself, he is every social man in his role opposite the grace of others; he is eminently the priest, but he is also every man who does not wish to say to God as he did Cain: "Am I my brother's keeper?"[6] Elisabeth Leseur wrote: "Every soul which lifts itself up, lifts the world! Every soul which lowers itself, lowers the world!"

This guilty man who knows himself to be a sinner humbly calls the other sinners, not to humble them or arrogantly judge them or raise their debts which they have incurred. Nor does he insult them by doubling or tripling their rents; he does not

[6] Gen. 4, 9.

175

demand "interest and capital." He is about to treat them as he would have the master treat him. He is going to act rather kindly towards them as though their sin appeared a small thing in his eyes. Generally, sinners perceive sin everywhere; they ascribe the same bad intentions to others which they themselves would have in such a situation. The unjust steward does not act like this. He does not want to see any more evil. He says: "How much do you owe my master?" He knows the amount owed, but he asks of each man what he thinks is owed in conscience. He knows that debts of this kind are not objective but subjective, that good as well as evil depends more on our interior choice than on the scale found in ethics books.

Some owe oil, others wheat; they have been anointed by the Holy Spirit; nourished by the Bread of Life, the Word of God. No creature lacks the unction of charity which is kindness, strength, and light. In fact, the oil soothes pain, makes the bodies of athletes supple and feeds fire so that it gives off light and heat. No creature lacks this essential food from him who has made everything, and through whom all is saved. It is not a question here of the Eucharist in its limited liturgical aspect, but rather of the great banquet of creation of which it is the sacrament. The Father gives himself equally through the Word and the Spirit. But men waste just to be wasting the gifts of the Father of light. . . .

The sinners whom the unjust steward calls together are not at the end of their tether as he is. They still have some chances for reparation. But the longer they wait the wider the gap spreads between what they receive and what they owe. They are not happy; they are in the grip of a guilt complex; their

176

debts weigh constantly upon their minds. What then is the unjust steward going to say to them? Fraternally received—yes, received as brothers in crime—they scarcely believe their ears: "Take your bill," declares the representative of divine justice. "Sit down, put yourself at ease, don't tremble so much and write! Make up another bill quickly, fifty barrels of oil, forty-eight of wheat. . . ." Fifty . . . forty-eight . . . why this discrepancy? Is it a special preference? We do not think so. At most the steward is lowering his neighbor's debt. The Word being made flesh . . . unto death—is the exigency any greater? Or, when it is a question of the Spirit of Love, does liberality come easier than when it is a question of Truth? Or is the essential bread more necessary than the oil of mercy? If somebody thinks differently, we shall be delighted to hear of it—he would have to be more expert in the symbolism of numbers than we are!

Whatever it may be, the unjust steward's audacity is to act as though he were the employer. He gives nothing, for he has nothing more; but he remits the debt of others, not those owed to him, but those which are owed the master! He does not give, but he forgives in the name of God. Did he claim a right which he has not got? Certainly, his actions are irregular, and in this respect he is doubly unfaithful, he increases his broken confidence but—and here comes the revelation of this parable—he has done well, he knew what he had to do to save himself. The master's praise is substantial proof of the fact. Here we find ourselves outside the realm of reason, justice, and equity, far removed from the world of the *Law* and in the paradoxical world of Charity—the kingdom of heaven.

Strictly speaking, because he himself is guilty he does not whitewash the guilt of others. A judge in court must deny himself any compromise with the criminal and enforce the legal code to the last iota even though his conscience is uneasy over it. Cheating, indulgence, making friends to the detriment of the moral law and especially of equity is never permitted in the universe of justice. Besides, Christ does not condone peculation, venality, and the buying of consciences. Such an application would take us back into a materialistic interpretation of this spiritual parable which raises us up into another universe that is entirely spiritual and whose sun is love.

Each sin of man's is ultimately the refusal of God. The prodigal son admits, "Father, I have sinned against heaven and before you."[7] And the Psalmist cries out in the *Miserere*: "Against you only have I sinned!"[8] Every sin against ourselves and society reflects back to God and violates the law of God's love, the law of true love. I injure my neighbor and it is God I have wronged. I borrow from my neighbor and it is to God that I owe. Love of God and love of our neighbor go together hand-in-hand, linked inseparably like the bottom and top of a sheet of paper. It is surely written that the debtors in oil and wheat owed God alone, but if, instead of wasting their goods like the steward, they had paid their debts, the steward would have been in a less difficult situation. We capitalize on all the mediocrities, villainies, indolences, and crimes of all men. In a certain fashion—either directly or indirectly—they whom the steward called owed him something in the same way as they

[7] Lk. 15, 18.
[8] Ps. 50, 6.

178

owed the master. They had placed him in the most awkward situation and he receives them kindly and unarrogantly in a "perfect" understanding of a common misfortune. Seeing the sins of others, he does not forget his personal sin. Humbly, he pardons for him and God, he does all he can. Of course, he cannot act as though there had been no fault, no debt. Evil is evil. But he is good and brings God's goodness into the case at hand. He makes an act of faith in this goodness. He involves God in this injustice crying for pardon. And God approves of it. God openly approves.

Judges according to Charity

God pardons and asks us to pardon—in his name, in the name of mankind. He goes so far as to make our pardon the condition of his. In judging others we must always take this fact into consideration; in being hard we must never plead for his justice; we must make ourselves responsible for his mercy. Why he, the Holy One, is placed into the hands of sinners in order to forgive them is a mystery, but there you have it. That he appealed to sinners to forgive and promised them the remission of the debts if they made this wisdom, this prudence their own, is sufficient proof that he is anxious above all things for the triumph of charity in men's hearts. He wants men to love themselves more. He wants their law to be an indulgent goodness, both patience and pardon. He desires that we make friends with our brother sinners, with all men. "Do not judge!"[9] Above all, do not condemn! On the contrary, be unjust. Do not take the facts or

[9] Mt. 7, 1–5; Lk. 6, 37.

179

intentions into consideration, leave that to my love. Act with love towards one another! And do it in my name.

As in this parable, it is more particularly what is owed to God, sins against him, and less directly about the sins against our neighbor, and since it is also a question of being accountable to God among men, we have here a precise enough application of the universal law of pardon. The Pharisees are the champions of God, but they forgot to look into the emptiness of their souls, into the decay of their whited sepulchers. They showed themselves ruthless spiritual masters before the little people and they even surcharged the law. They looked down their noses at sinners, and far from making the road back any easier, they pressed down upon the yoke. There are still, there always will be Pharisees. The priests to the Christian, the militant to the simple faithful, the believers to the pagans—they who, more or less, have charge of souls are often as hard as justice; they show God a pitiless face which they themselves would not like to confront on the Day of Judgment! If they think about their sins at all, they unleash themselves with still more fury against other sinners—as one guilty of a blunder in class tries to swerve the attention of a law teacher by denouncing another student as guilty as he, and as we have seen immediately after changes in government some collaborators try to excuse their villainy by drawing attention, more than their real partisans, to their fellows in the political upheaval. The mistake of these revengers of justice, the greatest sin of God's stewards, is to have acted without mercy. The unjust steward was not long in finding a solution to his personal problem of salvation, for he knew that

God is good. And all men are accountable to their brothers for the goodness of God.

The sacrament of penance is the evangelical institution which best corresponds to the teaching of this parable. The priest in the confessional is not a saint; it may be that he is even in grave sin. But his is the mission to forgive his brothers, to welcome them with tenderness and to forgive their sins. He is a man and he represents the God-man, he represents God and humanity. He remits the debts of men towards God and the human community. He is the image of God's mercy and offers his brothers that hope which alone will excite courage and allow the setting of things in order. Love alone can awaken justice. Not the opposite.

Let us leave the men of the Law shrugging their shoulders before the tribunal of pardon, let us leave the men of strict moral law to protest against this work of pardon which overflows from the confessional and extends to every aspect of human behavior. We know well that this is not an invitation to evil; for love calls upon love. And love pays off debts more easily than fear all the more so because our essential debt to God and our neighbor is to love Love, to respond to Goodness with our hearts.

Therefore, if we good stewards, knowing the price of infidelity to the Law and fidelity to Charity, knowing that with God it is not a question of justice, and if we wish to hope for redemption, we shall have peace in believing the Father forgives us as we forgive!

The Unmerciful Servant

THIS parable does not require extensive commentary. It is a continuation of the *unjust steward*, but its transposition to the spiritual register is much more easily accomplished. It makes no allusion to the subtle role of accountability among men or men inasmuch as they are responsible before God for their brothers, being invited to play the part of God in this world in the sense of pardon. Here it is not a question of the avengers of God or of inquisitional judges compelled to more pity by consideration of their misfortunes. . . .

Exploitation of God's Compassion

We are confronted with the question of judgment, God's and man's. God's judgment is not verbal, nothing of the kind: there must be a calling to account; one's entire life is set upon the scales. A man owes one thousand talents. He is a satisfied fellow whose life has borne no fruit, a man who did not know

182

how to make God debtor to him because he gave nothing to God beyond what the Law exacts. He is a man without love, or at any rate, a man of very little love! Justice does not waver in his case. This man weakened his potentiality for existence because he allowed earthly goods to harden him; he procured everything for himself and his family; he is a rich man. He wound up believing everything that God had entrusted to his care belonged to him. And in the judgment of justice everything is going to be pitilessly snatched from him; he is going to be bled dry. God's gifts are going to return to their proper owner. It is tragic to learn we have nothing when we thought we had everything. What a maddeningly dizzy plunge this sudden destitution is! Losing everything, giving everything back, the condemned servant feels the distress of his nothingness. Instead of wisely saying, "I deserve it. That's the way it goes. We must realize the obvious fact that man depends entirely on God. So I had more than my share—but we only truly possess what we have given—something ought to be left me. There is nothing. So much the worse for me!"—no, this sinner does not accept his lot. Instinctively, he flies to another kind of justice. Instinctively, he senses that the king was a good king. He always begs inside the area of his legal justice—like the prodigal son homeward bound. But he does not hit into the heart of the matter: he assuages himself by requesting a delay. He will pay. Yes, everything! Dimmed in his narrow perspective, he never arrives at the concept of a God who is love freely given; he cannot conceive of a charity transcending the bounds of human justice. Driven by fear and the desire to secure his happiness, smelling a weakness in the Divine, a blindspot in the Almighty God, and counting on his capacity, he "draws upon emotion" to gain some time, to blot out the problem . . . and the debts. "Have a little patience with me!"

The master took pity. Being God, how could he not but turn an eye of compassion on the mournful comedy of sinners who bank on God's being overly generous, who put off till later the necessary efforts to correspond to the generosity of grace? God knows that the man who frees himself from his love actually becomes prisoner in a closed-in universe of an egotism that makes barren and eventually kills. No half-hearted measure will free him from this prison, but only the full measure of God— an absolute measure. When God forgives, he re-creates, he sets up a new order after first overturning the old. Everything shares anew in the warmth of his love. By an unprecedented generosity, he lets the guilty go—that is, he gives him back spiritual freedom—he has absolved all his debts however large they might be.

Such a gesture would crush egotism, would open a sinner's heart to the revelation of a transcendent economy, to an order whose law is liberality. "Who can but love him who has loved us so generously?", sings the liturgy of the passion. But how many minds can accept what surpasses them? They look for earthly explanations in the most munificent of actions. Always blinded by their false riches they interpret selfish, sordid motives, even trickery, in the most spontaneous and most generous of actions. They cannot believe in love because they are incapable of love.

The Unmerciful Man

This man does not for an instant believe in a true and permanent pardon. Will not God one day re-demand the payment of incurred debts? He cannot forget his plan of delay which bears the imprint of human wisdom mixed with a little benevolence. And barely gone away from his master he meets one of his companions in debt to him for a few denarii. What man is there whose brothers do not owe him something—but who himself does not owe them? God, in pardoning the offenses to his glory, does not at the same time pardon the sins against our neighbor, for they are the same faults under two aspects. God has forgiven everything in his name and in the name of all men—those at least who accept the aid of charity. The debtor is not one of these generous souls! Barely forgiven his debt, he goes out and throttles his brother who owes him very little, so little that it is better not to mention it. Sins against God have an infinite repercussion; even when we view sin from the human aspect and its human repercussions, the worst is still a little thing, as is everything in the created order.

"Pay what you owe me!", he cries out while strangling him with his greedy fists that were clenched to take and which fists have not learned to open themselves up to liberality . . . as they who love open their hands, their arms, their hearts to make the union possible—as did Jesus upon the cross. With what rage this man who has just benefited from so much kindness demands his rights—he who has never fulfilled his obligations! He is getting justice and more than that, for the justice of the rich is an exploitation and, to be refused the excess from above, it must give itself over freely to those here on earth. The right of the stronger is not an empty word. The Law of justice quickly becomes that of Cain and Lamech: "I kill a man for wounding me, a youth for bruising me. If Cain shall be avenged sevenfold, Lamech seventy times sevenfold."[1] Jesus, however, told Peter who in his generosity was willing to parden seven times over: "I do not say to you seven times, but seventy times seven."[2] The parable in question is but an illustration of his statement.

Not only then does the hardened heart desire all things for itself, not only does the forgiven debtor take back what was owed him, but he does so with the cruelest severity. This one has no compassion! Not this beast! He is not like the king who allows himself to be sponged off and weakens at the sight of a few tears! Satisfied, he pockets the denarii. However, the scandalous contrast of Law and Charity cry out for his condemnation. Charity alone creates solidarity between men. The spiritual Mystical Body is only such in the light of love. Egotism, sin divide. The wicked will never form themselves into a mystical body of evil, but only coalitions of interests, convergences of hatreds. They are allies ever ready to jump at each other's throat. Men are always prepared to accuse. It is not solely a question of virtuous indignation in the face of evil. Christ himself wielded the whip and he did not recommend the preachers to cudgel abuses with silk fans. But it is a question of the indignation of the Pharisees, those great defenders of morality, those whited sepulchers, and the indignation of all who, burdened with debts,

[1] Gen. 4, 23–24.
[2] Mt. 18, 21–22.

are jealous of the fortunes of those whom they showed all appearance of "befriending."

God's Justice

He who wants justice will have justice in order to judge. The servant in this parable is dragged a second time before the master because he did not believe in love, because he was not receptive to love, because he was not alive: "Wicked servant, I forgave you all the debt, because you entreated me. Should you not also have had pity on your fellow servant, even as I had pity on you?"[3] By demanding what was owed to him, he lost every right to indulgence. He lost everything, everything he wanted to save from what he possessed only too much. The Gospel is clear: Driven by rage, he hands him over to the executors of justice.

In the "Our Father" we ask that our sins may be forgiven as we forgive those who sin against us. Our Father will treat each one of us, his sons, according to the way we pardon our brothers "from the depths of our hearts,"[4] that is, totally in feeling and in thought . . . today we would be more inclined to say: to forgive with no ulterior motive: according to the Hebrews, the heart was a tribune of judgment!

We find no bargaining here: "If you forgive, I shall forgive you."[5] Who would invite men to play the comedy of pardon in order to be pardoned themselves? A pardon from deep within

[3] Mt. 18, 32–33.
[4] Mt. 18, 32–33.
[5] Lk. 6, 38.

our heart is not just any pardon. It is a question of true charity and not of selfish motives. Now, we all know that it is heroic and superhuman to forgive, to show ourselves understanding, to put ourselves in another's position, the position of the accused . . . ; what man is there who reinstates his brother into the union of friendship after a grave injustice as though nothing had happened? What man, after having forgiven, accepts his brother with his incorrigible character, shortcomings, idiosyncrasies, and his human injustice? For, by original sin we are all fundamentally unjust before God and our neighbor.

The truth is that there are two incompatible worlds—the world of the Law and the world of Love. He who lives in the world of hard, implacable justice, though being compassionate, submits to its laws even as he overcomes some others there. He who, on the contrary, enters into the world of charity, is forgiven to the degree that he forgives.

The Rich Man and Lazarus

LUKE 16, 19–31

THIS parable is found in St. Luke whom we know had no special love for the rich. It is not necessary to conclude that this was a little personal idiosyncrasy of this excellent physician. . . . St. Matthew was no less favorable to this particular class of society. For, if he does not emphasize the light of the beatitudes by the darkness of curses, "But woe to you rich! for you are now having your comfort!"[1] he does not forget the dilemma of the Sermon on the Mount: "God or mammon!"[2] and he tells the other parable of the last judgment which is such a threat to the privileged of this world.[3]

Christ judges the rich severely; that is obvious. His example corroborates his teaching: he manifestly chose the poor. And it is with pain that we think not only of the unfortunate, but of the affluent societies, our own in particular, where comfort and worldly devices are being constantly perfected while all about

[1] Lk. 6, 24.
[2] Mt. 6, 24; Lk. 16, 13.
[3] Mt. 25, 31–46.

us millions of people die from hunger in those countries a puritanical language terms the "underdeveloped areas." . . .

Indeed, there are loopholes. We have recourse to the spirit of poverty in the midst of wealth, that spirit of mercy which permits us to turn the mammon of iniquity into a means of acquiring friends in order to welcome them into heaven: a kind of simony through almsgiving. There is mystery in a rich man. We sense infernal predestination in him, and in the "good rich" we encounter a fearful pity. Does not fate under the guise of temporal happiness offer them eternal damnation?

The Rich Man Wicked through Omission

In Christ's parable the wicked rich man is not called "wicked," but merely "the rich man." If it is recounted that Lazarus desired to fill himself off the crumbs of the banquet table, it is not mentioned that they were refused him. And why would he have kept coming back to the same place if he had not gotten something from it? Personally, we have thought for a long time that the sin of the rich man lay in his inattention and ignorance of the poor man's existence. He did him no harm, but he still did not consider him; he had no compassion. We never fail to stress our obligation to be concerned with our neighbor; we single out the fact that in our neighborhood, sometimes in our very homes, there live unfortunate people whose financial, material, or moral state is tragic. We do nothing for them because we think only of ourselves. Egotism blinds us to our brothers. We leave them to die, not by direct acts of cruelty, but by excessive adulation of ourselves or of those we love. Our vision is narrowed and we have forgotten our responsibilities. If we could be witnesses of their plight on our very doorstep, our hearts would be overwhelmed and through compassion our soul would accomplish the imperious task of solidarity. The unforgotten poor whom we have placed in the central light of our preoccupations would excite us to scrutiny and they would save us! Is there not an element of solution here? We must keep our eye on the poor, for it is the same as paying attention to Christ himself. We must love the poor, for then we are loving Christ himself. This identification is necessary and in it we have one aspect of this love of God and neighbor which is the only one commandment with two faces.

The Rich Man Wicked through Possession

But must we not love the rich also? The poor man sees him as his enemy and often he is actually the enemy, for sometimes the rich exploit the poor, even though the rich man is not wicked. Now, it is said we must love our enemy . . . and the rich man lives in such an environment of greed and vices, or at least has at hand the ability of doing evil with the minimum of risk— for with money he may buy everything, even souls—the rich man, though he be not a sinner, belongs to the world of sin and is so inextricably connected with injustice that he seems to have a right, as every man, to redemption. Christ, in fact, went down to the home of Zachaeus and showed a predilection for the rich who renounced their goods and became themselves poor in order to follow him.[4] Let us note in passing that this is not

[4] Lk. 19, 1–10; 18, 18–20.

enough to be poor like the cynics of ancient Greece, but we have also got to follow the Saviour—and by the narrow path.[5]

Christ blames the Pharisees, those purists of the law, and often of modest fortunes; he blames them more than the rich publicans. He willingly goes to their houses, partakes of their feasts to the extent that his enemies treated him as a drunkard and contrasted him unflatteringly to John the Baptist, the renowned eater of locusts and husks! The "worthy men"—like the Pharisees —all murmured, "This man welcomes sinners and eats with them." But Christ justifies himself: "The publicans are also children of Abraham![6] [In our parable Abraham calls the condemned rich man "my son"!] The Son of man has come to look for and to save what was lost."[7]

Consequently, the rich can be saved, and their salvation lies in generosity and the giving up of their goods. The wealthy are not abandoned by the Saviour who loves them as he loves the poor, for he places the greater part of the blame on the Law! In addition, is it not surprising that Christ did not investigate slavery and preach revolution any more than revolt against the Romans? Yet three centuries passed with edicts forbidding the branding of men marked with the seal of his love. St. Peter recommends obedience not only to good masters, but also to the strict![8] The established order—often an established disorder, set up by the rich who have the power or the powerful who have the wealth in capitalistic or communistic states—does not primarily or directly interest Christ. Then how can we explain

---

[5] Mt. 19, 21.
[6] Lk. 15, 2; Lk. 19, 7.
[7] Lk. 10, 9–10.
[8] 1 Pet. 2, 18.

these attacks upon the wealthy and riches? How can we explain this parable we choose to study which contrasts the rich and poor purely, simply, and radically?

If it comes to that we may read the following: "For it is easier for a camel to pass through the eye of a needle, than for a rich man to enter the kingdom of God"[9] . . . especially if we expand the eye into a city gate. (All the same! Let there be some to pass through so that all may set their minds at rest!). . . . We refer to the possibilities of salvation which are still open to us and which are, as we have said, almsgiving, and what is better, the abandonment of wealth. But the parable—as the text of the curse—places on Abraham's fatherly lips some disgustingly unjust remarks: "Son, remember that you in your lifetime have received good things, and Lazarus in like manner evil things; but now here he is comforted whereas you are tormented,"[10] and the torment is eternal and unceasing. An abyss gapes open where charity itself cannot pass between the rich man damned because he took pleasure in a little earthly happiness—eternally damned—and between the poor man who had the misfortune to be unhappy a few years upon earth. Evidently, nothing is more consoling to the poor, nothing better invites them to accept their misery and to amuse themselves in their plight with an eternal revenge.

The Truly Evil Rich Man

In other parables the rich man is the image of God. But here we must recognize that in our parable transposition the rich man cannot enjoy the position of favor accorded the unjust

[9] Lk. 18, 25.
[10] Lk. 16, 25.

steward, and we must recognize that he is not to be congratulated or imitated: he is irremediably lost. Therefore, the rich man is not the positive symbol of the fullness of divine values, but the negative symbol of another kind of fullness which is void of God. In the extreme, he is the idol mammon, incompatible to the God of Charity; he is Antichrist. The story invites us not to envisage a limited case, but instead the spiritual case of him who is mammon incarnate on earth, who partakes of puffed-up nothingness and the foolish semblance of existence. As it is in fact nothingness the rich man possesses, thus what is condemned is a spirit, a finality of the spirit.

The costly gloss of a rich man is the captation for himself of all created values, a "centripetal" spirit which throws the world and the ego out of balance to seal them away from divine attraction and give them over to the idol of egotism and pride. So the poor man at death was drawn up into heaven, carried by the angels into the bosom of Abraham, and the rich man was buried in hell.[11] Each one receives the merits of his life accordingly as he gave himself up to divine realities or to earthly vanities. Our freedom consists in our giving or taking; we have got to give ourselves over to God and through him we conquer the universe: our slavery becomes the freedom of the children of God, the flowering of a liberated freedom delivered from and relieved of the adhesive goods of earth. If we choose created values, if our appetite only settles upon base ambitions, we shall find ourselves ensnared by what we possess; we shall fall victim to the temporal and ephemeral. What we give frees us, what we possess traps us.

Certainly, money is a great spiritual threat, being as it is the

[11] Lk. 16, 22.

principal of the slavery of ourselves and ours. That is why money typifies all goods to which we attach ourselves and in which we disperse ourselves and lose our interior unity, the meaning of our life. In reality it is easy enough to be cleansed of the common riches; but besides them there are other riches of intelligence, imagination, esthetic feeling; there is thought and beauty, there is the heart and so many human affections, not necessarily carnal, but valued too much. "Blessed are the poor in spirit!"[12] This does not only mean "Blessed are they who, even in their wealth, have the spirit of poverty!" That is too remote from the boldness devoutly cloaked by our modern exegetes: "Blessed are the poor in spirit! It is a question not only of being poor in wealth, but also, and especially, in spirit!" Do we admire willingly, as the Christians of the past, the severely mentally retarded magnificently called the "simple"? Who does not admire the family whose mentally retarded child is considered a blessing? The misfits of earth are behind their splendor. "Now," one father said at the death of his retarded child, "I have a son like the others!" This son who took no part in anything human was valued more than the others, and because he had only the love of God, he contained all God's love which is the only beauty, the only truth and wealth. The poor in spirit are a disturbing presence in the bosom of our society of proud science: poor parents in the family make the parvenu blush for shame! But this offensive, ill-smelling presence signifies other riches in the scandal it causes. That is why there are always scandals and poor people on earth—people poor in all categories: poor in lands, luxury, and foods, poor in memory and reason, in taste, in culture, and in reputation.

[12] Mt. 5, 3.

The First Beatitude

People brought to this awareness must not reshape our patterns of behavior and upset the apple cart of our false security. They must carry out the first beatitude—the one on poverty—which makes ready in us a special place where the fiery tornado of the Holy Spirit can surge. The mystics who suffer the night of the senses and the spirit know what it is like for they tragically endure the experience of their radical nothingness so that Christ, the way to the kingdom of heaven, may be made present. "Blessed are they who are cleansed of every dross of creation, for theirs is the kingdom of heaven." God could not find shelter in the inns at Bethlehem because they were filled. The poor man is always the detached one. He walks in truth because a created being by itself is nothing; it must recognize its nothingness, it must test its dependence. The poor man begs, relies entirely on those to whom he reaches out his hand. The rich man has no need of others; he is his master and the master of those who have nothing. The attitude of the property owner, the wealthy owner, is a delusion, a revolt, a breaking-away on the part of the created being. While the Creator gives himself to those who return again to the source of their existence, who are living "yes's," he will refuse himself to those occupied with themselves and their goods which are actually stolen from God since they declare and make themselves masters over them. But as soon as the creative influx is removed, nature becomes bloodless and wastes away; the bubble bursts. That is the way of goods separated from God. They swell up the proud egotist. They are bits of nothingness and he who feeds on them is himself empty. A sorry banquet for one weakened by eternal hunger. But God fills the hungry with eternal good. "Open wide your mouth and I shall feed you."[13] Paul Claudel compares this mouth opened wide to the mouth of a communicant, a living "yes" which we are about to utter; for the mouth is opened distinctly to form the word "yes!"[14]

Wealth—of the body, senses, thought, heart—distracts from God, diverts our attention from the one who is the uniquely Necessary One who nourished the contemplative Mary. The rich man does not concern himself over the poor or over the Poor Man begging the love of men with outstretched arms and an open heart. The wealthy man thinks of the earth as an agent for pleasure; he builds a Babel and always unsatisfied he ceaselessly raises up his pretensions. The rich man does not know how to curb his desires; being created for the Infinite, the nothingness he seeks and possesses crumbles in him as in a bottomless pit ... which the pagans symbolized by the thunder of the Danaïdes. The insatiable desire of earth-bound men is a sign of the nothingness which wells up within them—the lack of God to satisfy them with his plenitude. Because they live for the present, because their outlook is cramped and they do not know how to look for the Absolute alone which is worth all the trouble, and because they desire to surrender themselves to their lot in life and their happiness, they are proudly incapable of obtaining what man cannot earn, but only receive: that is, to be and to increase according to nature and grace. In this perspective the rich man is naturally evil and the poor man good. The rich man

[13] Ps. 81 (80), 9; Ez. 2, 8.
[14] *Positions et Propositions*, t. 2, p. 168.

is the Godless man; the poor man is the God-man, at least a man
divinized by Charity.

Incompatibility of the Rich and the Poor

The poor man on earth has need of earthly sustenance; but the
crumbs of the rich, the insignificant things[15] are enough for him.
Little does he care that the mighty and superb have monopolized
all things so long as the absolute minimum of worldly goods is
allowed him to live out his earthly pilgrimage. It is no great
thing to him if even this little bit is begrudged him in the plan
of the eternal; the kingdom of heaven already within him is
revealed to his soul in the ecstasy of boundless Joy. The lot of the
man who has not utilized creation as a lease-holder, renter, or
custodian in God's service is death, a grievous death, the tearing
away of the being who is by nature oriented to God and whom
a perverse will has directed and has never ceased directing
towards creation. The impulse of the created being inspires the
appeal "Father Abraham!"[16] When he has nothing more, he
comes to realize his dependence on God. God, who will answer
him through Abraham, will not ignore him: "My Son."[17] We
can guess at Christ's infinite distress because the young rich man
does not want to follow him simply because he has no desire to
forsake what death will pitilessly snatch away from him! He
spoke with the same tone of voice to Judas holding the thirty
pieces of silver, exchanging his God for a little money, a little

[15] Lk. 16, 21.
[16] Lk. 16, 24.
[17] Lk. 16, 25.

human security and the diabolical thrill of possessing things. "My friend . . ."[18] The real night of despair, empty of the promise of resurrection, has taken hold of him.[19] Christ himself could do nothing about it: "My friend, is this how you betray me?" Judas threw his money away; death sweeps everything aside; it is too late.

Had Judas still been capable of loving, Christ's word would have been efficacious and he would have quickened and responded to that love, were it only by so much as a single fibre of his heart. The rich man's words do not express any regret, any feeling of repentance, not the least affection for Lazarus; he was not humble, neither was he receptive to God and his glory. He thought only of himself. He continued his unaltered life of egotism and looked upon Lazarus as a flunky at the service of his happiness. He was not even ashamed to ask the intervention of the one man he crushed with his false grandeurs and deprived of the humblest of rights. "Father Abraham, have pity on me, and send Lazarus to dip the tip of his finger in water and cool my tongue, for I am tormented in this flame." The illustration of fire is particularly well chosen, for it signifies perpetual destruction, the devouring of one who on earth had destroyed in order to feed his hunger, who was sated on others, who made the world his prey. This curse without so much as a single drop of water is perfect!

Death arrests the impulse of a creature; and it remains fixed forever; it emerges into the present which has no tomorrow and affirms the meaning of its evolution at its death. But the one

[18] Mt. 26, 50.
[19] Jn. 13, 30.

damned knows just as the elect what it is about; he is certain what he ought to have believed. The rich man appealing to Lazarus is a sign of this conscience enlightened by what it ought to have done on earth. Then Lazarus needed only a few scraps of food to subsist; his terrestrial condition required few goods to which his spirituality conferred a positive sense of directing the impulses of his soul to eternal riches. The rich man, in order to be saved, had a very real need of Lazarus. The rich man's sin did not lie in beating or refusing provisions to the poor here on earth. He forgot about Lazarus because he was filled up with himself and his empty riches. And in not paying attention to the wretched beggar, he did not perceive that Lazarus was infinitely more wealthy than he; he did not see that he would have to beg from him that one drop of water which sustains life and quenches thirst, satisfies desires and brings happiness. He should have looked to the poor man to offer him less an offered hand than a too empty heart. The poor man might have given up his heaven for that. As Lazarus is poverty personified, let us say that the salvation of the rich man would have been his turning to poverty, the first of the beatitudes, the gate of the beatitudes, the entrance way into heaven. Had he renounced his goods or had he detached himself from them, and having recognized the true riches, he would have obtained them not by taking them, but by the gift of himself. He might have begun here on earth the mystical process of deprivation: *todo y nada!* The wonderful example of St. Francis of Assisi comes to mind. The son of a great merchant, celebrated and esteemed, he wrapped his naked body in the rich cope of God's gifts; he espoused Lady Poverty. He was the *Poverello* who had lost everything—money and glory: he became a poor man and a fool . . . he tried to seem as much madman as pauper. He distrusted the learned as much as the rich and did not want anyone in his family who prided himself upon his culture . . . and yet he was a refined man and a noteworthy poet. He taught the humble Brother Leo the secret of perfect joy: ". . . and now let us suppose that, driven by hunger, cold, and the encroaching darkness, we knock once again upon the door and with burning tears implore the Brother Porter to allow us entry . . . and let us further suppose that he becomes greatly enraged . . . and throws us onto the ground, rolls us in the snow, and overcomes us! Ah! But if we endure all that . . . convinced that it is good for us to suffer for love of Christ, Oh Brother Leo, hear me well, therein would lie the perfect joy!" We find in this "flower" of St. Francis not only the renouncement of pleasures, but even the welcome and happiness of those whom we love: the fraternal monastery is closed to the poor man who, in the quandary of earthly happinesses, is brought to look above for something which he discovers as the threshold of true happiness!

The rich man can only enter into dialogue with the poor man if he uses the goods of earth as means and not ends. Wealth and poverty on the spiritual level are as opposite as materialism and spiritualism, as two contradictory perspectives upon the use of worldly values. It is quite normal that at death, when ultimately the rich man emburdened by his wealth, and the poor man with his poverty, and abashed with their divinity, should find their rewards so antithetical because all communication between them is impossible: "And besides all that, between us and you a great gulf is fixed, so that they who wish to pass over from this side

to you cannot, and they cannot cross from your side to us."
There is no lack of charity in Lazarus, just as there is no lack
of charity in the wise virgins who refuse their oil to the foolish
ones. There are two orders of realities which cannot intersect,
and accordingly as men take one boat or the other to cross
opposite banks of a river, it is possible or it is not possible for
them to remain in communication. The fate of each one is just,
for each man has chosen his lot. One has desired to receive his
goods during his lifetime; the other has accepted his sufferings.
They have it in their power to change their existence on earth;
the proof of it lies in the rich man's appeal for mercy on his
brothers: "If someone from the dead goes to them, they will
repent."[20] If he has lived in the closed world of passing goods,
shut off from all visitations of grace, it is because he did not
want to hear the voice of Moses or the prophets. . . . And yet
certain prophets like Amos were not hesitant in crying out
against them: "Bulls of Basan . . . you oppressors of the poor
. . . depart from your wickedness!"[21]

If we recriminate against the disproportion between temporal
pleasures and eternal pain, between the misfortunes of a day
and the everlasting joy when the merciful God of the Apocalypse
will himself dry the tears of the poor—with such gentleness!—
when he will turn a deaf ear to the howlings of the damned,
we must not forget that the kingdoms of heaven and hell begin
invisibly here on earth in the hearts of the poor and the spiritually
rich. Neither must we lose sight of the fact that we are not
concerned with quantity, with the weight and measure of our

[20] Lk. 16, 30.
[21] Am. 4, 1; 6–7. See Ez. 33, 17–20.

202

sins, but with the option of our life, the choice of freedom which is either given or refused. In the same way we must not forget that we are concerned with the rich-type or the poor-type, that is, with men who serve as examples through their total adhesion to hollow riches or to filling poverty. And the men who waver between good and evil for the most part, will be accorded the eternal destiny they merited, being judged by God's love which is perfectly just and God's justice which is perfectly good . . . and, of course, their underlying intentions will count more than their apparent acts or visible situations! Let the poor eaten with jealousy, hoping to usurp the place of the rich, take care! Let us know how to find our joy in being nothing, deprived and despised!

Grace and the Rich Man

The condemned rich man's supplication[22] begging a miraculous intervention from Lazarus in behalf of his five brothers cannot be considered as the appearance of a charitable feeling. The outlook of the condemned man is outside the evangelical spirit which is centered upon love and not happiness. "For he who would save his life will lose it; but he who loses his life for my sake will find it."[23] That is the spiritual paradox. He who gives up his most intimate possession, himself, will receive the smile of joy with the countenance of his God upon his face. The condemned rich man lost all he had because he was obsessed with the thought of getting: he would have gotten hold of

[22] Lk. 16, 27–28.
[23] Mt. 16, 25.

203

God or would have sold him to others if he but knew how! Had he been given God, it would have been like a purchased something!

This passage of the parable is concerned with showing rather that the terrible damnation of the rich man was not the result of a fate cruelly predestined by God. The revelations of God and the graces dispensed to all are largely sufficient to convince the rich man of the inanity of his pleasures and his "hoarding up." Death is the best messenger, the most illuminating angel of God! It is enough to reflect a moment upon death which ravages all things if we are to understand the vanity of all those goods to which man attaches so bewildering a value. Where is the man who would willingly at this moment desire the obligatory renouncement in order to have in his hands the richness of voluntary sacrifices? However, the rich are blind and deaf: their senses are jammed and blocked; they are living unyielding "refusals" to the love which gives everything! Only the poor can be evangelized, for—spiritually speaking—they are the overtures to God.

The rich man who is thus named because he is concerned only with himself is closed to salvation, to the degree that he is rich. "If they do not hearken to Moses and the prophets, they will not believe even if someone rises from the dead."[24] They are hardened to such a point that the Lazarus returning from the dead would be no more persuasive than the Lazarus living at their door! "Go back where you came from!" these men glutted on Pharisaism, these proud adorers of the pitiless Law would shout and sneer as they scoffed at, rejected, and killed the

[24] Lk. 16, 31.

Divine Pauper with a violent death—he who was so wonderfully gentle.

In truth, the supplication of the rich man was heard. God joined the New Testament to the Old, and, from now on, the renewed Poor One's shadow falls across the path of the happy on earth as a loving reproach, a permanent invitation and supreme hope for salvation.

But the rich go on filling the earth and continue their daily carousings at the expense of others and the death of God. They have already introduced hell in their realm. And there they will stay when the Holy Spirit comes to fill the banquet halls of heaven with all the destitute who wait for their cross at the crossroads of their life!

The Invited

MATTHEW 22, 1–14
LUKE 16, 16–24

IT is not a question here of comparing St. Matthew's text[1] with St. Luke's[2] in order to argue over the vocabulary differences under the pretext that the one mentions a king and the other a man. Whether it be a question of the wedding feast in honor of the king's son, or of a great supper, we must bear in mind that it is always the kingdom of heaven where love is shared as is the bread; they are spiritual *agapēs* where one soul is united to other souls in a mystical communion to the Son, and by him to the Trinity.

We enter into the heat of the battle against the Pharisees, and we can see the discourteous invited ones as the leaders of people who believe they have the right to dispose of God and all privileges themselves, and they are ultimately excluded from the kingdom of charity and true happiness which their pride does not accept. Thus, from the historical approach, it is possible to

[1] Mt. 22, 1–14.
[2] Lk. 14, 16–24.

206

see the Chosen People's abandonment of the real Promised Land, the Son of God.

Those Invited to Awareness

But Christ, in this anecdotal story, surpassing earthly contingencies, struck out against Pharisaism. Against our own. He surely told this parable several times under slightly different forms. But we are positive he did not mean to censure the purchasing of fields and their inspection! Nor did he condemn the ploughman for trying his oxen, and the newlyweds for taking their honeymoon. He did not reproach them for the inopportunity of their actions, since they were most reasonable. And it would not be sufficient to conclude this discussion of the parable by stating it is admirable to buy, to plough, and to marry, but we must not do these things instead of going to Sunday Mass which, as we all know, is an obligation under pain of mortal sin!

One can accomplish every temporal task—and here he must consecrate it—and at the same time, and by the very act, answer the call of the Master. We have got to include the fields and their vegetables, the oxen and the plough, the newlyweds and wedding festivities in the kingdom of heaven, and bring the entire world to the feast which lacks guests. God is going to summon the evildoers, the unfortunate, and the idle.

Those who ignore God's invitation, and who, angered at Love's insistence, destroy graces coming to them, even that very grace meant fully to develop their beings, are the "rich," the possessors of this world, the spirits riveted to their goods and worldly preoccupations. They live for their selfish interests, their pride, ambitions, their feelings. They are so filled up with themselves and ephemeral values, intellectual or otherwise, that there is no place in them for the things of God, for the "fatted animals," for the heavenly foods most enriched in love, the richest goods, genuinely rich with eternity!

Claudel wrote to the sick: "You are those who, like the invited of the parable, have been constrained to enter. Either permanently or temporarily, you are those invited to watch.* Are you sure that all the people standing around, moving and active, whom you envy, are you sure that they live as intensely as you? . . . Does not a bouquet of beautiful fresh flowers, a platter filled up and overflowing with great bunches of grapes bring more joy at the bedside of a sick man than upon a Parisian coffee table? . . ." The sick are invited to a higher communion, "to consent to God," to lend "an ear to this insistent and personal calling."[3] People who do not suffer do not come into contact, do not listen—those who act, assess, buy up, those loaded down with lands, animals, servants, whose egos hide their existence, they are the ones deaf to the invitations from heaven, blind to what is hidden to the great and revealed to the humble. Their attention, which is the notice of their spirit, the orientation of their existence, is elsewhere absorbed. It is fixed upon matter, not upon the heights, and here we must refer to the parable of the rich man and Lazarus.

The task of those invited to awareness is to close themselves

---

* ". . . invited to watch." The true meaning of this phrase, *"invités à l'attention,"* is best expressed by the Latin: *"Vocati ad exspectandum."* It denotes a passive part, but an interior alert, an interior awareness or attention (translator's note).

[3] *Positions et propositions,* t. II, pp. 249–250.

off from the turmoil of the world, to shut themselves in their interior chambers, to expel from it all thoughts or learned vanities —even theological by nature—their passions and especially the obsession of the ego. Like Mary, in absolute contemplation, they can then hear the voice from above and nothing will hinder them from ascending into the ecstasy of love. Worldly goods in themselves are not evil; they are often signs from God, invitations to the praise of the Creator. But their selfish possession sets up a wall between God and man.

The poet who has nothing goes his way freely and sings of God in nature which is like a sacred display case of God. But how many are not, in Pascal's phrase, distracted from God? The distraction which the giddy kaleidoscope of the modern world provokes most often prevents us from corresponding to a divine generosity that excludes no one. Modern civilization rises up like a Babel without God, and no one can any longer understand what is going on, neither can they hear. He who listens to the Spirit of Pentecost can make himself understood, like Peter, to all men. The language of charity is accessible to all who know how to listen, and the true Christian civilization is built upon this unity. Is attention to the spiritual still possible on our chaotic planet, and is not religious activism one more noise in which vanity resounds, harmonizing with the instinct for power? How can we understand that they who desire to hear the essential message at any cost hide themselves away like the hermits of yesterday in retreats, or better in contemplative monasteries?

In this parable the poor in spirit are symbolized by all comers, by the mass of "anyone-regardless-of-whom," not by the obdurate in their own glory and happiness, their own implacable ideas, their personal ways of doing things, their sectarian fanaticism, and all who seek a spirituality centered upon the eminence of their spiritual dignity by the "acquisition" of holiness (what a lofty expansion of the ego!) "I want to be holy!" We must give even that up, for it is God who wants us to be holy. We have got to love God with the love of children, to go out and lose ourselves in him, and then holiness is accorded without the pride of possessing it, because holiness is God and we cannot own him. He does the calling, he asks us to come, and he fills us with his joy. The first prerequisite is to pay no attention to anything but him. The poor, the crippled, the blind, the lame, everyone who lacks something, needs something, everyone who stretches out his hands. What an imploring and attentive gaze the beggar casts upon one who can provide him for what he lacks! St. Matthew even incorporates the wicked in his list,[4] for sinners are called, invited; they will even be assisted forcibly if necessary! There is no prayer in which the sinner begs God to constrain his too weak freedom, his imprisoning liberty. It is enough to "desire" to respond to the appeal, even though one "cannot." Therefore, sinners are called and they even have priority. The wicked . . . and the good! But the help of God, the grace of heaven, will not act upon their wills if they do nothing on their part. It is not important whether they come from the city or the crossroads, the market places or from the streets and waysides. They are outside: they have no home; they have no goods: everything is possible for them; they can all hope! If they worked the ground, if they persisted doggedly, if they busied themselves (we have to occupy ourselves well), if

[4] Mt. 22, 10.

they were totally committed in the absorbing affairs of the earth, devoted to money and their positions, to their studies, their loves, and even to their religious pride, they would not lift up their heads in answer to the messenger's appeal. God is dead within them in the sense that his voice, his word, is dead in them. They who are available to grace, who are not attached to the world, can be saved; they are imperiously shoved into the banquet hall.

The Robe of Love

There is another condition. The "wedding garment" is said to be another parable. Were it placed in any section whatever of the Gospels, it would still be one with the parable of the invited ones.[5] It is useless to make a great issue over the customs of those banquets: nothing has been left us by science to document. Let us simply note that in the *prodigal son*, the most beautiful robe was given him, upon his return home, at the same time as the ring was presented to him. This is the garment which symbolizes the state of the soul, just as the white garment does at baptism. *In albis!* The exterior signifies the interior. The prodigal son had regained his lost purity, his filial character, and his state of grace. Here the wedding garment typifies charity, the spiritual marriage . . . and not the works of justice or faith. We are concerned with the crowning of the life of that soul which knew how to detach itself from passing goods, which was able to hear the divine calling and was able to respond to it, and which now fulfills its noble destiny in the spiritual union (and we may say that it was a question of the invited one's

[5] Mt. 22, 2.

marriage). Who is more invited to a wedding than one of the spouses? It is a question of the spouse, the king's son; the spouses are the poor souls. Thus, in the parable of the virgins, the spouses are the virgins themselves. The spouses in our parable here are the beggars, the crippled, the idle, that is, those who do no longer believe in the horizontal domain where economical and political values hold sway, they who give up the material world and all that subtly fills a man up with himself, satisfies him with religious complacency . . . the latter especially, because it is the worst, being a contamination and inversion of the best!

However, sometimes it happens that the chosen one who has renounced the world, and now poor, though receptive, though prepared to receive his God as he is received by him, is incapable of loving. Though he has renounced the world and destroyed his "ego," he did it out of disgust, feeling keenly the nothingness of all things. Now the evangelical mentality is quite something else: if we must die, it is to be brought back to life again and this dying to be resurrected is accepted on the cross of Christ. "Go and sell all that you have and follow me!" We have to renounce, but we can never despise creation—which is valuable all the same in relation to the Creator—we must give up these things for the love of God. And this creation is found in God, positive and illuminated by heaven!

The whole parable of St. Matthew forms a single unit from the invitation to the theme of the wedding garment. Confronted with appeals for grace, the reactions of the soul are signified therein with their eternal consequences. The parable begins with a rich perspective and ends with a grave threat: the rejected one is bound hand and foot, the final state of bondage for all who desired to be freed of God: they are made prisoner of their hollow possessions, separated from their true "ego," the "divine image," and distant from God himself, kept from their happiness, eternally thrown off their center of balance, and they end up in the darkness after having taken pleasure in the false lights of the idol chosen on earth . . . far removed from the God of Light, they lie in the abyss of their nothingness.

If we have so easily separated the second part of the parable from the first, it is because we wanted to favor an historical interpretation which is not without interest because of its proximity to the parable of the vine-dressers.[6] But if the messengers are the prophets whom the Chosen People—the sons of the Law—rejected even to killing them, it is not a question of the immolation of the Messiah, the son of the king. And is it truly necessary to see the pagan or Gentile everywhere in the destitute? Do we have to believe that the burning of the city—an image of hell, an image of the hell that is a world without God—was the foretelling of the destruction of Jerusalem?

For our part, we take exception to this interpretation, and without forcibly attacking it, we see in this parable the manifestation of an assiduous and attentive love accorded to all men— whether they are receptive to it or not. The severity of the agony corresponds to the generosity of the call to divine intimacy; it is not a punishment, but a tragic consequence of refusal. It depends on every chosen being. The conditions are not to be obsessed by the possession of the created so that they may be *attentive* to God, as in the salvation of men. But—as Péguy said—it is not enough not to love creatures in order to love the Creator. Re-

[6] Mt. 21, 33–44.

213

nouncement is one stage of the spiritual life. To have any worth it must be polarized by the charity in which it will find its plenitude. He who disdains the finite, preferring the infinite, is still a calculating Pharisee. He wisely selects the true, lasting, and perfect happiness. But this spiritual egotist who bursts into the courts of heaven as his home because he thought it more preferable to give up the fields, his women, or the idleness of street corners, this egotist who does not love God without loving the world, who loves nothing but his own personal happiness, will be driven from the banquet hall. If we are to gain entry into the eternal wedding feast, the mystical union of heaven, it is absolutely essential that we love!

Conclusion

An exegesis of the chief parables helps us better to understand the revealing importance of the disturbing or astonishing incidents in these stories so familiar to us. We should also have been able to comment thus on the parable of the weeds sown among the wheat.[1] What shocks us is the workmen's bewilderment in face of the weeds, and their naïve question, "Will you have us go and gather them up?" Farmers certainly know that weeds grow among the wheat and that one cannot gather them up before the harvest, because, if one does, then the remedy becomes worse than the evil. When we transpose this to the spiritual plane, as Christ did, we see that the good always gives rise to the question: "Why is there evil in creation?" Evil depends on the initiative of the evil spirit which is a fact in a creation where freedom exists. As there is no negligence here, evil is manifested as inherent to the rhythm of the world, its negative counterpart (sleep) alternating with the positive (daily toil). The necessity of allowing the weeds to grow up with the good crop proves still more clearly the necessary presence of evil in the evolution

[1] Mt. 13, 24–30, 36–43.

215

of creation on its way to its final goal. Evil is thus free and necessary. As long as evil remains, the problem of the struggle is present: "How can we get rid of it?" Surely, Christians would be in favor of a kind of surgical operation that would give them the hope of basking here on earth in an idyllic virtue. But the spiritual dialectic is struggle: progress is possible only through victory and the overcoming of obstacles. The wheat requires a victory if it is not to be choked out so it can grow with more vigor, absorb nutrition from the soil more voraciously, and lift its ear of wheat higher to the sun and further away from the passions below. What would charity be if egotism were not possible? The field of God is a courageous field and only the spiritually strong at harvest time are worthy of the eternal garnering. Here, once again, we have made full use of our method of spiritual anagogy.

The Spiritual Struggle

In addition, we have everywhere encountered the most subtle and bitterest essential struggle between the spirit of evil and the Spirit of God, not only the flesh's battle against the spirit, but the Law's against Charity. The flesh is not an evil in itself. It becomes, like money, the occasion or consecration of the downfall of the proud spirit. To illustrate this crucial struggle more clearly, Christ did not allude to the battle between atheism or paganism and the true faith. When he speaks of the faith of a mustard seed,[2] let us not see it as a prideful development of charity which has at least accomplished the most to give all souls happiness and well being. The Church is as indispensable

[2] Mt. 13, 31–32.

as Christ, whether it be glorious or conquered, and rather victim than victor with a handful of martyrs than with a legion of Constantines or Mazarins. Christ is indispensable and his failure is his glory. The Church's temptation is to desire its numerical ascendancy. But it is most important that it make Christ present here on earth so that here it will permit the action and diffusion of the Holy Spirit in order that all its suffering and death at the end of the world, with Christ, may be redeeming for humanity, as the seed of his Body gives birth and increase to the universal spiritual Church.

In any event, sinners and pagans are not vilified by the Gospel, and if mammon is chosen, it is a question, as we have seen, of egotism which is the possessive closing-off of the creature to the open generosity of Charity. We reinstate the spiritual order. So as not to appear to be offering here any presumptuous statements, we refer to the reading of the parable about the rich man's avarice.[3] Someone from the crowd asks Christ to decide a question of inheritance. Christ refuses to intervene on the social plane just as he has always refused intervention on the political. He offers the spiritual principle which is sufficient to engender equitable solutions on the earthly level. How could one who aspires to truly eternal values be unjust in the division of ephemeral goods? If men preoccupy themselves and fight each other for such vanities, it is because their hearts are there. "Take heed and guard yourselves from all covetousness, for a man's life does not consist in the abundance of his possessions."[4] The whole bulk of temporal wealth is not worth one tiny act of charity. The parable clearly succeeds in stressing the nothingness

[3] Lk. 12, 13–21.
[4] Lk. 12, 15.

of riches (it is not said that they were evilly acquired). They are such a little thing that he who has nothing but them at the hour of his death has got nothing at all. The foolish rich man is condemned, not because he was rich, but because he hoarded up treasures "for himself" and was not "rich in the sight of God,"[5] he was not rich *for* God: he did not love! The conclusion to this parable is significant: on one hand we have egotism, on the other charity. We see once again that the essential plan and wealth of earthly goods, such as the flesh or the world, only appear evil by their disquieting interference in the spiritual "magnetic field." If the Gospel curses mammon and its fellow travelers, it does so because they are the starting points and influences tending towards evil, certainly, but more so because they sound the downfall of the soul without God, the soul impoverished by the loss of heaven! This dissolution is already a state of condemnation: hell has begun!

Christ, wanting to situate the spiritual struggle on his own terms, stripped the fundamental truth of all that is false, and consequently, the senses. That is why Christ and sectarian Pharisaism, the Gospel and the Law, are at grips with each other, proudly rebellious. The parable of the Pharisee and publican praying at the same hour in the temple, but with strikingly different attitudes, perfectly symbolizes this radical opposition existing between two orders of life, though both might be "religious," in the same practice and faith.[6] Prayer is the test which makes the distinction between the sons of light and the sons of darkness possible. Any other situation or action, because temporal, includes an ambiguous something which confounds judgment.

[5] Lk. 12, 21.
[6] Lk. 18, 9–14.

The intentions here cannot appear complex, divided, or camouflaged. A definite opposition exists, but it is not between those who pray and those who do not; it is between the overt and covert attitude of souls. We are aware that whether these souls are in rapport with their neighbor or with God, it is actually the same thing. Rapport with God is essential and it assumes all the others. There is found in this parable a complacent, self-centered, "self-sufficient" attitude which decrees rights and separates the individual from what is not himself, whether it be a question of one superior to him (whom he treats as an equal), or whether it be a question of those either equal or inferior to him (whom he regards haughtily as objects to be dominated). The other attitude is open humility to the welcome, the welcome of God and neighbor, and all who can and desire to give. Everyone whose love is spiritually rich will not be refused or rebuffed. The first attitude fixes the man and drapes him in his outrageous sovereignty: it would humiliate the Creator if he could not laugh at such cheek. The Pharisee declares himself an ally of God. His representation is more odious than an enemy who meets the Eternal face to face, for he pretends that this God he does not need must pray for him and come to his assistance. The publican does not humiliate God; he recognizes his absolute need for his love; he alone knows how to pray; only he can obtain the Lord's grace.

Divine Life

Now we may analyze the allegory of the vine which St. John offers us in the discourse after the Last Supper.[7] We shall not dwell long on it, for one can find excellent commentaries on this

[7] Jn. 15, 1–11.

text everywhere. Besides, we are not concerned about confronting the Law with Charity except insofar as the Law separates and deprives these vines of the sap of love: the Law, we well know, when it is only a dead growth upon a tree trunk, when it is only the letter, lignifies and hardens souls for eternal fires.

Before, in the parable of the barren fig tree, we made allusion to this part of St. John which it strongly resembles. Here the Father is the vine-dresser and Christ is the vine, the true vine, that is, the living vine, meaning the one heavy with fruit. What is a doctrine that is not alive? The Word of God is not a philosophy, or even a theology, it is a person who loves, who gives himself, who enlightens and vivifies.

The symbols from the barren fig tree to the True Vine seem to make no impression. For the goal, here, is to insist upon the interiority of grace. Christ is no longer the one who digs around, fertilizes, and looks after the soul. Because he was accepted, because he dealt with a receptive soul who prays to have life, he slips into that soul and becomes its food which is so little accidental to it that it becomes one with the soul who accepts it. Is not the mystery of the Eucharist the fact that man is devoured by the Bread he received? Thus the soul is no longer the vine, but Christ, the soul of souls, if we dare use this expression. It is the prerogative of the superior Living One to assimilate the inferior living being. But this assimilation is not annihilation. It is exultation. Divinization. Not for one soul only, but for all who do not refuse this sap, this unique sap, the unique life. It results in the assumption of all faithful souls into the transcendent unity of this Christ whose sap, or divine grace, whose life irrigates them for the fruits of charity. The entire doctrine of the

Mystical Body is summed up in this wonderful page of the Gospel. If the Law is damnation, Charity is eternal salvation—a salvation which is not an outward gesture to a piece of flotsam, but a blazing presence in the heart of men—paradise already!

The proud, the Pharisees who wish to live in no other being but themselves, even though that being were God, may band together as a sect, a religious community, a Christian party. But theirs is no true Church, no Mystical Body, no spiritual community. The humble alone can unite themselves with God, integrally link themselves with him; and by the power of the grace of charity infused in their spirit they share in the community, the family of the sons of God. They become "new men" who can do good, for they may ask "for anything they wish."[8] In fact, they desire no part of anything which is not the Word who dwells within them, who was made flesh and who sacrifices himself. Their action speaks. Their life, rescued from self-centeredness, is given to respond to the divine gift and to be conformed to his law in favor of the human community. When this circumincession of Charity into the Mystical Body has been accomplished, this prelude to the eternal pleroma, there will only remain the consummation of the creative and redemptive will of the Father.[9]

Prayer of the Poor Man and the Importunate Friend

Such is the proposed salvation. The joy of the life of charity in God stands in opposition to the Law. Such an ardent hope must

[8] Jn. 15, 7.
[9] Jn. 15, 11.

be acquired, or rather begged for. In the *Pharisee and the publican* we considered prayer as an experimental field better to illustrate the difference between the Law and Charity to which this entire book is dedicated. It is well for us to conclude with a prayer strong in hope. The overture to God (or to the most high being, if one does not yet believe) is primordial; it conditions the prayer of salvation for us and for our brethren, mankind.

The parable of the *importunate friend*[10] shows what the prayer of the sinner, the poor man, can do, that persevering prayer which will only fully be heard at the end of our life in the full kingdom of the Spirit . . . and it shows especially what the prayer of charity can accomplish. For it is this last aspect of prayer which is essential to this picturesque parable. We have not stressed it quite sufficiently! We have noticed only the amusing scene of the untimely friend who inconveniences his more fortunate friend who has some bread, who has even got "three" loaves, the perfect food. In fact, this splendid parable is about prayer for other people. It takes place between friends.

A faithful heart is the friend of God, this God who is eternally in act or lies dormant, whose presence is felt in the groove of the history of the world and in the history of souls; the heart of the believer is close to the immanent Distant One, close to the transcendent Present One. And this heart of the son of God is moved because his brother has no bread, no bread which satisfies in the night of terrestrial existence, in this empty night, this night of the only real absence: the sin of nothingness. In this world without love, men go hungry, and then it happens that they turn their minds to the true bearers of the Gospel. They reach them by long,

[10] Lk. 11, 5–9.

222

profoundly moving spiritual and dramatic voyages, pilgrimages of salvation. Provided that they encounter genuine Christians, and not Pharisees, but receptive, fraternal, and understanding souls! If these souls know how to pray, not for themselves, and if they can forget themselves for the starved beggars of the spirit, then salvation is promised them. Still, these souls must possess the humility not to pretend to nourish others with their own abundance, their own theological wisdom, their own ideas, and their own interior riches. We have got nothing we have not received; we exist, we have value only through God. Open to his grace, we can be flaming lights of his Light. If then someone comes to us, it is neither to worship us nor to depend on our gifts, but to encounter Absolute Love, the Source of Love through us.

"Ask and you shall receive! Knock and it will be opened to you!" And here are so many worthy people who take God for a St. Anthony of Padua, and this exemplary saint for a charlatan kindred to card-trick fortune tellers and fakirs. They go in search of lost objects; but they do not even dream of their lost soul, and those lost souls! They neglect reading to the end of the sacred text: "Therefore, if you, evil as you are, know how to give good gifts to your children, how much more will your heavenly Father give the Good Spirit to those who ask him!"[11] Elsewhere, the spirit of holiness gives place to the spirit of goodness.[12] Charity is always the Spirit of Love. This is what is not refused: the Father will not refuse it to us if we do not cease asking it for our brothers, mankind; for it is in saving others that we save our-

[11] Lk. 11, 13.
[12] Mt. 7, 11.

223

selves. The preoccupation of a Christian must be the same as Christ: to bring lost sheep back into the fold! If our minds are turned towards this goal, if they vibrate with charity, if they are lost in love, then evil—the worst kind, egotism, spiritual pride—evil, we say, will not hold any sway over us. Thinking, living, acting with the thought, the life, the action of the Saviour, our hearts and minds with him, we shall be saved with him . . . and this is to be saved in saving others!

On condition that there is not excessive introspection, an introspective humility awakens from the knowledge of God. This awareness of God may even shake the angels, the Church, and all things established.[13] By our prayer we must awaken to God, and with him the whole of creation. True prayer unhinges both heaven and earth. The conversion of a single soul is a revolution. It alters everything and opens wide the way for total joy.

It is our hope that far-off souls in quest of Truth and Love, generous mendicant souls who are searching, who possess all the means necessary—particularly God—, it is our hope that they may find in these pages not merely an expounding theologian or exegete, but a heart praying only to be the humble mediator of God's grace!

[13] Lk. 11, 7.